MY PANDEMIC PARADOX
A surprising development from this calamity.

By Lynn Zimmering, May 2020 - May 2021

TABLE OF CONTENTS

SECTION THREE: TIPS ON HOW TO LIVE BETTER

ISBN 13: 978-1-942500-73-5
Boulevard Books
The New Face of Publishing
www.BoulevardBooks.org

INTRODUCTION

Starting in May, 2020, due to COVID-19, when I was laid off from my part/time job, on my 88th birthday, I found myself with nothing to do. Painful! I spent time doing jigsaw puzzles, watching TV in the middle of the afternoon and taking naps. It was miserable. It's difficult enough being quarantined with one's family, but living alone as I do, it's downright solitary. So, I started writing my feelings in the blog format and continued each week to find another topic to delve into. Somehow, writing about my history and focusing on one thing at a time, I was able to close many troublesome (and some happy) memories of my life and times. My goal was to write 50 of these stories and publish them. And, here they are. It's my hope that you, reading them, might relate to some of my issues with some of yours.

Even now, after my double-dose vaccine, I'm still mainly at home. My daily outing is going to the lobby of my high-rise for my mail. So, that leaves me with 23.75 hours free. Deduct eight hours for sleeping (if I'm lucky), two hours for food preparation and eating, one to two hours for jigsaw puzzles, what's left is at least twelve hours to be filled every day. Writing blogs has saved me from the weariness of empty hours.

I've not been a serious writer in the past but have done some writing at former jobs. I was a Supervisor in the Call Center at Unilever for several years and did some writing while I worked there. Our phone reps used an online manual to give clear, correct, and concise information to our callers. Unilever was introducing a new product line, and I volunteered to write its manual. I was surprised that I got the assignment.

I realized that people's use of language is very imprecise. During my phone rep years, I answered many consumer calls in which I had to guess what the person was talking about. Bottles could be referred to as cans or shampoos as suds, for example.

My official introduction to writing was that product manual. I needed to make sure that my language said precisely what I meant it to say. I asked myself exactly that question, "Does this sentence express my thoughts accurately?" and if the answer were "no," I would rewrite it. I still do that in my blog writing.

I use a blog site, Medium.com, to post my blogs. As blog sites go, Medium is easy to handle. It is my habit to write a new blog each week. Around Tuesday or Wednesday, I start worrying about my next blog topic; by Thursday, I make a choice and start, mentally, adding flesh to the theme. Friday is research and first draft day. Saturday and Sunday, it's rewriting, rewriting. And then rewrite, again. I read the blogs out loud over and over to make sure they sound smooth. I use a Thesaurus when I'm stuck for a word and Unsplash.com for my photos.

Creating these articles is the best way to fill my time. It's engrossing on every level, fun, creative, intellectually challenging, and has an inherent sense of accomplishment. I've achieved my goal of creating a legacy, wrote fifty blogs (so far) and will have created a book to give away to my family and friends. I've done the writing. Now, it's the publishing hurdle to jump over. I'm thrilled that I've been able to get this far. Fifty blogs is a body of work. Who knows, maybe there will be a Volume II.

I hope you find these articles as seeds of life that may help you gain new insights into your experiences.

DEDICATION

*Life isn't about
waiting for the storm to pass,
it's about
learning how to dance in the rain.*

– Vivian Greene

SECTION ONE: GROWING UP

Man's main task in life is to give birth to himself,
to become what he potentially is.

– Erich Fromm

ALL ABOUT MY FEELINGS
How it feels to live alone.

Can it be that another day has passed, another week, and soon another month. My world gets narrower and narrower by the day. How come I'm not reacting to these changes emotionally? How is it that I'm not frightened? Each day of my pandemic confinement in my apartment is pleasant and cozy.

I question and feel guilty about my shallowness. I don't share with friends and family that I'm enjoying being home. It embarrasses me.

I was brought up to be disciplined, positive, and cheerful; never allowed to experience feelings, good or bad. I heard over and over, **"You are not entitled to feel that way, young lady."**

I concluded that my feelings were wrong and I didn't deserve to feel things. Was that possible? So I buried them inside. I was a GOOD girl. If I achieved excellence, it was not acknowledged with pride. In fact, it was barely acknowledged at all. I was invisible as long as my mood was obedient. Can it be that this lesson is still resonating with me (even after all my therapy?)

Intellectually, I fully understand that we are in great danger of becoming deathly ill ourselves, losing our loved ones, losing large amounts of our savings. Security has all but vanished. Traditions are abandoned. Our future, no matter how few years may be left to us, is cloudy.

Where is my anxiety? How far down is it buried for me to feel it?

Sometimes I get a clue that something is going on in the depths of my being. The other day, the muscles around my left eye started twitching. The twitching is gone now. My neck is so stiff I can hardly turn my head. Occasionally and unexpectedly, tears come to my eyes, like now.

I don't know why.

Could it be that the lessons of my growing up years are responsible for my deficit of emotion? Or is it maybe not a deficit of emotion but rather a deficit of awareness of my true emotional state? Or, is this something I'm supposed to overcome?

Sometimes, I am thankful for having been taught these control lessons, and sometimes I am proud of my disciplined and cheerful exterior. These qualities have served me well in the terrible times of my life.

DOES COMPETITION BLOW YOUR MIND?
How being competitive changed my life experiences.

Competition significantly changed my life. I grew up in a competitive environment, and maybe you did, too. It's significant to consider what some great philosophers had to say on the subject. Competition has been studied in every aspect of life.

Every time I find myself in a room with strangers, I compete with them for dominance. I don't want to, but I can't help myself. I want to be the most educated and the sharpest. While on the surface, I appear relaxed and eager to please; inside, I'm a cauldron of anxiety.

Am I at the top, middle, or bottom of the heap? If I'm at the top, nothing further needs to happen. If not, I have the patience to listen carefully and when the moment is right to say something that will boost my position.

It's a drag but a necessity for me. I think it has to do with survival.

The logical next question would be: What would happen to me if I am not or at least near the top? I don't know the answer.

Mahatma Gandhi

Gandhi speaks of egoistic competition. For him, such qualities glorified and/or left unbridled can lead to violence, conflict, discord, and destructiveness. Parmeshwari Dayal, Gandhian Theory of Social Reconstruction, Atlantic Publishers & Dist, 2006

Gandhi's explanation makes sense to me and may shed some light on why, if I'm not at the top, it may cause my ultimate destruction, or it could lead to being ignored into oblivion.

I seem to have been introduced to competition at a very early age.

I grew up with a cousin who is my age and whose father and mine were in nonstop competition with each other over us. Their underlying competition remains a mystery, maybe even to them, if they were still alive, but its observable characteristics dealt with my cousin and my accomplishments.

Although we were very different, we were compared to each other in every way. She was a better student than I was, so she became known as the "smart" one. I took that to mean that I was stupid!

I excelled at things that I could perform, like dance and music. So, I became the "pretty" one. That meant to her she was not pretty or talented. The comparisons never ended.

To my father, I was as near perfect as a person could be. She was the same in her father's eyes. The odd thing is that our mothers were sisters, naturally in competition with each other, and our fathers only were related to each other by marriage.

Karl Marx

Karl Marx felt that "Capitalism encourages a climate of competitive egoism and individualism," with competition for jobs and competition between employees. Buchanan, Allen E. (1982). Marx and Justice: The Radical Critique of Liberalism.

Maybe our fathers competed with each other business-wise and buried their competitiveness in our successes and failures. Their issues may have been who was more successful and had the greater buying power. Therefore, which daughter would end up as life's winner mattered.

Instead of acknowledging we had different skills, my skill-set gain caused her loss. Or vice-versa.

There were only two possible outcomes. One of the combatants was the winner; therefore, the other was the loser. It's no wonder that I am always seeking a top tier. What fun is being a loser? My father would be so disappointed!

Is it possible that my success enhanced his ultimate prize, being the winner? It could be explained if he secretly viewed himself as the economic loser in his competition with his brother-in-law? Who's to know that answer?

Karen Horney

Karen Horney's Theories on Neurosis deal with the highly aggressive, competitive personality type, characterized as "moving against people." In her view, some people need to compete and win at all costs as a means of maintaining their self-worth. Hypercompetitive individuals generally believe that "winning is so important, it's the only thing that matters." Ryckman, R. M.; Thornton, B.; Butler, J. C. (1994). "Personality correlates of the hypercompetitive attitude scale: Validity tests of Horney's theory of neurosis." Journal of Personality Assessment. 62 (1): 84–94.

My father was a big man with a big personality. He was always at the center of his world, loud, funny, handsome, and smart.

He made all the family's children laugh by acting goofy. He was an assistant cook in the US Navy in WWI, so our laugh sessions were often in the kitchen. He would cook or bake something that somehow rocketed out of the bowl and landed on every other kitchen surface — the floor, the countertop, and even sometimes, the ceiling. We were always giggling at his antics and loved being around him. It's hard to think of him as an intense competitor, but, thinking back, at heart, I believe he was.

Competition has been studied in every field. Family dynamics is certainly one of them. This trait's ramifications are in every family's history and can underscore how a family behaves. It can also be a factor in diplomacy between nations. How different would the world look today if the competition for wealth, land, and power was not such a motivator?

Another unanswerable question.

DOES YOUR HAIR HAVE HISTORY?

To men and women alike, hair matters.

Here's what we do to hair: wash, condition, style, brush, dye, shave, remove by laser, or electrolysis, or wax, pluck, tweeze, and thread. There are so many ways to style it, too many to name, but here are a few:

Guys sometimes have Mohawks, flat-tops, bowl cuts, comb-overs, or go bald, and girls have braids, updo, or the famous pompadour worn by both men and women. We wear wigs and toupees — all in the service of looking good or other valid reasons.

Hair must have something special about it. So I researched and found it a symbol of power, fertility, identity, and pride in how we look. It has religious and cultural significance. We develop group identification through our hairstyle and conform to religious teachings by covering it.

Check out Wikipedia on "Hair." There is a vast amount of literature on the subject of hair.

So, it's not just hair. It's MY hair.

My mother takes me to have my first haircut at Best's and Co. department store when I'm two. I throw up (or so I am told) as soon as I feel the cold-bladed scissor on my neck. I must be so terrified. (That is the last haircut attempt until I am thirteen years old.)

Shirley Temple, the child movie star, is a style-setter in my early years, and we both have curly hair. That's about where our likeness ends.

The new Shirley Temple style for little girls is to have big fat curls instead of the cork-screw type. For me, that means standing very still some Saturday morning while my mother impatiently brushes my curls around her fingers, pulling my hair unmercifully to make the appropriate style. This fussing is in preparation for having lunch with my father and his male friends. We do that about once a month. Mom is jealous since she is not invited to these outings. So, she lays into me by yanking my hair around. I need these curls, however, to resemble Shirley Temple.

We frequently have lobsters at these lunches! I love lobster, so I ignore the preparation discomfort. I'm about four to five years old and too little to object. I learn to accept whatever comes my way.

Other than Saturdays and holidays, my hair is in braids. That hurts, too, from the tightness of the twist.

Something has to be done about my growing hair where it doesn't belong — on my face. I have a unibrow and a shadow of a mustache. As a preteen, this hair affliction is a horror for my mother, and I am embarrassed, too.

Mom finds me an electrologist downtown, who rescues me and my face. It is an acceptable treatment for the removal of misplaced hair. Each week, I take the subway downtown to her studio, alone, for a treatment. The treatments are agonizing.

Hair mustn't be in the wrong place. It has to go.

A needle is poked into the root of each offending hair follicle (this hurts), to which an electric charge is administered (this hurts even more), killing that particular hair. This is done one hair at a time. By the time the treatment is over, the area worked on, my brow and my upper lip, are bright red and hot.

The electrologist then puts calamine lotion (it's pure white) on my face, and I walk through the streets and take the subway to get home. My face looks ghoulish. I am scrutinized by every single person who sees me. They stare, and I pray to vanish. Then, next week, I do it all over again. I am thirteen years old. The treatments work, however. The unwanted hair slowly disappears.

By my high school years, I take care of my hair myself. Thursday night is hair night. In these years, we only wash our hair once a week, so Thursday is it. I shave my legs and my armpits, too. Since I still have a mustache's vague shadow, I bleach the shadow, all on Thursday night. It feels like a necessity.

After college, I met a guy who I think is divine. One night, at a gathering during which we all have a lot of wine (I have scotch), he kisses me. That is also divine. Then he says, "I could really go for you, but you have too much hair on your arms." What? Once again, hair causes me pain, this time not physical but adding to my already impaired self-image. I end up feeling guilty and powerless over this disfigurement.

Since I'm so hairy all over, my head hair is really thick, dark, and curly. It's the only hairy attribute I like. However, by the time I'm in my late thirties, I see the first uninvited gray strands appearing. I always felt redheads had power. (This is based on Maureen O'Sullivan's role in some movies.) I dye my hair reddish to cover the gray and to give me an artificial sense of strength.

It looks good, so I keep the color for years, and I feel more "in charge."

Then, I become a Type 1 Diabetic, and ironically, my hair begins to disappear, all on its own, not only on my head but every other place on my body. After so many years of fretting about my hair, too much of it in the wrong places, too much work to take care of it, causing lots of pain to remove it, and messing up my love life, it's leaving my body: goodbye and good riddance.

Soon, I see smooth arms, legs, and armpits. I don't have to shave anything or continue dying my hair. I let it go totally gray. My hair issues have made a complete turnaround in my life, going from being painful and embarrassing to nothing at all. Finally, my hair issues are gone.

Except, of course, I still spend a bunch of money on what's left of it to have it cut and styled.

It's my hair, after all, and how I look.

GROWING UP IN HALF A ROOM
My teenage years offered me no privacy.

It always amazes me; I offered almost no resistance to my childhood living quarters. No matter how small the room or how big I was at the time, someone was always stealing my solitude.

I was an only child for seven years until my brother was born. We lived in a two-bedroom apartment in the Bronx. During my early years, my parents had the luxury of having live-in help. Of course, the aid had to sleep somewhere, so it was in my room. It didn't make so much difference to me since I was so young. The first girl was named Mary, and as a young child, I thought all the subsequent help was also called Mary.

So I named them all Mary.

Fast forward to my teen years, during which time we had moved to another two-bedroom apartment, this time in Washington Heights, the upper tip of Manhattan. The idea was to live in an area serviced by the "A" train (the best and newest subway.)

At first, my brother, who is emotionally handicapped, lived in my parent's bedroom, the larger of the two. When we no longer had a live-in aid, I had the smaller bedroom to myself. I loved that.

However, as soon as my mother felt that I was competent enough to take care of him (he was three, I was ten), I became his primary caregiver, and I moved into the more oversized bedroom with him.

Christmas time reminds me of these years:

My parents are toy wholesalers, so I see little of them from Labor Day until New Year's Eve. That means that every afternoon after my school day ends, I pick up my brother from nursery school, entertain him all afternoon, make dinner for him and myself, and put him to bed.

Chanukah comes and goes with no notice. It doesn't matter. My mother has escaped from caring for my brother and me into my father's business.

His nursery school teacher treats me as a parent, explaining to me everything wrong with him. My heart goes out to him, and I love him. I try my hardest to fix his problems, of course, to no avail. I carry that burden even today.

Taking care of him is suffocating me.

My friends know that wherever we go or whatever we are doing, my brother comes along. One time we all decided to take off our tops and bras to see who's new breasts' jiggled more when we danced topless. I had to bar him from the room by shoving a chair under the doorknob. I feel guilty, not because of the bare breasts, but because I feel I may have hurt his feelings by excluding him.

I realized I was not allowed to enjoy privacy in these pre-teenage years. My brother and I lived with each other in the same bedroom. My brother is always there and always chitter-chattering at me. He exasperates me every day.

When I start menstruating, my parents know they have to make some changes.

I need a domain of my own. Unfortunately, their business is failing, so we can't move to bigger quarters. Instead, Mom and Dad have a wooden partition built, dividing our bedroom into two spaces. I have already found my secret garden inside my head where I live, most of the time, but I appreciate their effort.

The partition doesn't go to the ceiling but is high enough not to see over. Each side has a window and ends up about 6 feet wide. The partition is long enough to accommodate a bed, and there is an area inside the open doorway with no division making for easy access to both sides from the room's entryway. The partitions have no doors that can create privacy on either side. It is as if my parents are allowing me some special haven but not too great a one. After all, I am still in charge of my brother, and I can still hear him across this barrier. So, I set a boundary. He is banned from speaking to me after eight P.M.

I need something in that space to comfort myself. I happen upon a series of Henri Matisse paintings on postcards and buy them with my allowance.

I attach them with pushpins to my side of the partition where I can see them lying in bed. The beauty of these works of art draws me into another sphere of colors, shapes, and intricate patterns, each combining to create a new world. I transport myself temporarily and enter into it. That world is where beauty existed. I cling to the hope of rescuing myself to live there permanently.

Finally, I go to college, and it's a great relief to be away, although I continue to worry about how my brother is doing. He is doing poorly. I graduate, and afterward, instead of then moving to an apartment, I return to my half of our bedroom. It is clear that my parents need me at home, and my mother and father want me back.

Unique circumstances create unique people. The old saying holds, true for me, "If something difficult doesn't kill you, it adds to your strength."

HAS COVID TURNED ME INTO A JIGSAW JUNKIE?
It's satisfying to fit those pieces together.

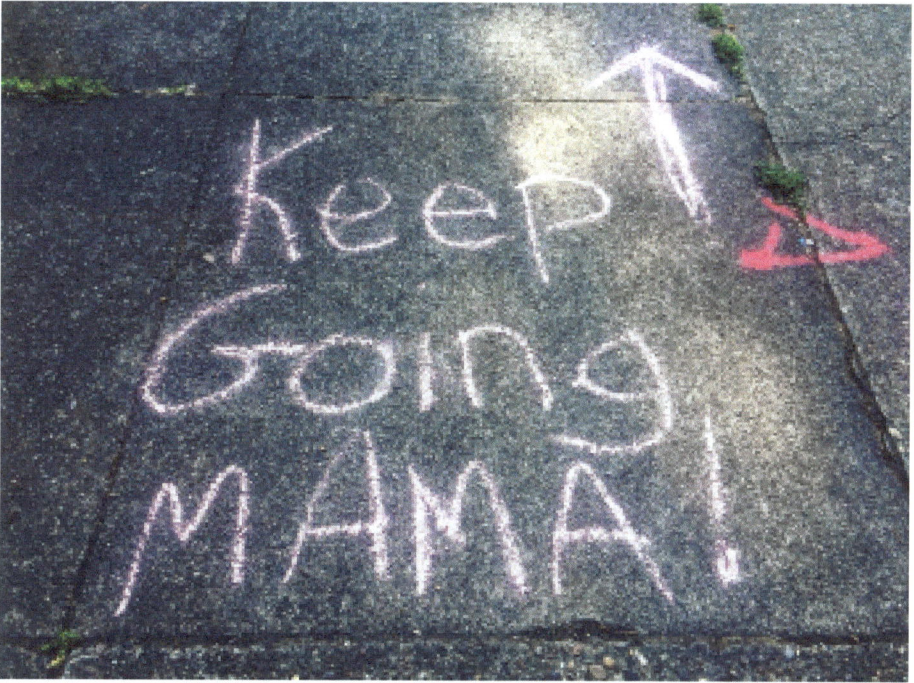

What do you do every day to fill up your time? Some days, I have nothing on my calendar and boredom takes over.

Well, that's not exactly true. It just feels that way.

Being laid off from my part-time job, trying to protect myself from being exposed to COVID by staying home, and having so much less contact with my friends and family, life can be very monotonous. Travel is unthinkable. It's a question of how to remedy this problem of nothing to do before I completely lose sanity.

Being 88 doesn't help, either!

What does help is reaching back into my childhood and remembering the fun I had doing jigsaw puzzles. Every Spring, I suffered from bronchitis and had to stay in bed. When my mother asked what I needed to make the time go faster, I could have said a book, but I always said a jigsaw puzzle.

I needed a flat surface and used a removable, flat, slide-out shelf that was part of the kitchen cabinetry, a perfect board for a jigsaw puzzle. And, I was good to go.

I loved the whole set-up. It almost made being sick something to look forward to!

Having something to do has always been my style.

My family moved from one apartment to another for various reasons. And moving was fine with me. Rather than being afraid, I was excited to go to a new school. It held my interest and certainly gave me something to do. Exploring new neighborhoods was fun.

That was except when I was ready to learn long division in third grade and feared that the new school had already finished that unit. Then I'd be in trouble. I was afraid I would never learn long division, and this deficit would haunt my future. Luckily, the new school was about to start the long division unit. Whew!

As I grew up, there was always something new on the horizon. Summertime was reliable when I either went to sleepaway camp or a bungalow colony in the Catskills.

During the rest of the year, there were Jewish Holidays to celebrate, someone's birthday, homework to hand in, dance recitals, and all sorts of other ventures keeping me busy. I really didn't have time for jigsaws.

As a newly married woman, my husband and I moved three times in our first two years. You can imagine how busy that made me. By the time we had been married for five years, we had three children under five years old. Not a single empty calendar day in those years.

I thrived on the activity presented to me.

It was only when my children got somewhat older and we moved back to the New York City area from Providence, R.I., that I began to search for new pursuits. They were busy with school and friends and I was lonely and bored. That's how I ended up with a Master's Degree in Experimental Psychology; it was a new pursuit. I had to keep moving.

I tried filling life with shopping, but it wasn't gripping enough!

Shopping is fun and can fill up lots of calendar days. But it requires lots of money. Doing jigsaws seemed, at that point, a total waste of time, and I never even thought about them. So, instead, I got a job.

My next project kept me very occupied. I divorced my first husband. That was an experience I never want to repeat, no matter how bored I became.

Time went on. I changed jobs, changed husbands, changed where I lived.

My second husband and I built a Berkshire vacation home in Massachusetts. There was plenty to do during the construction phase, and it was exciting to watch it take shape. It was on a lake and beautiful both on the inside and from the outside. Its tranquility was only interrupted by the sound of other people's jet skis darted around our waterfront. We eventually incorporated that sound as part of the lake environment, and it was OK.

We spent a lot of time at this house, and after I finished the daily weeding of my garden, I needed something to do.

Our bedroom had three windows overlooking the lake. We set up a portable table in front of the windows and did (no surprise, here) jigsaw puzzles on it. We either examined their shape or matched their color. When we found a piece that fit, it was satisfying. Hours flew by, as did our life together. Sadly, he passed away a few years after we sold the house.

I remained in the apartment we shared, but eventually, two years ago, I moved from that three-bedroom apartment to my current two-bedroom space in the same building. Mostly my friends and family couldn't believe I had the interest and energy to do this. After all, I was 86 at the time and, you know, moving is a hard job. But, I needed a new activity, and I had plenty of help from my kids, now grown, and their support was empowering.

And now...

I have settled into my new space, am unemployed, single, old, and with nothing to do. Just a few months ago, I had great activities that I loved doing: working, acting classes, flute lessons, play reading, classes at Bergen Community College for seniors, NJ Symphony concert series, and social times with friends and family, all now gone due to Covid-19.

Oh, no! COVID is spoiling my precious remaining time on earth.

I began to be aware of feeling very sorry for myself. Instead of continuing along that path, I tried to think of fun things to do while remaining in my apartment. Yes, I'm sure you guessed it.

I started doing jigsaw puzzles again.

I buy 1000 piece puzzles from Amazon. It's fun selecting which to do next. I lay them out on my dining room table. These days no one comes to dinner, so it's the perfect spot.

I've learned by reviewing my life until now that if something goes wrong in my existence, it's up to me to fix it. My happiness is dependent on my actions, and, for me, jigsaw puzzles seem to be the perfect vehicle. Yours may be something entirely different. Who cares if I have become a JIGSAW JUNKY?

I believe it's a benefit for everyone to take responsibility for their own lives. It's not fair to expect your happiness to come from other people. Joy and excitement are personally available to us at whatever level we can handle — each of us chooses how to hang out. There are no rehearsals for how we live each day. Do-overs don't exist.

IS BEING PASSIVE NATIVE, OR MUST IT BE LEARNED?
An exploration of my most humiliating trait.

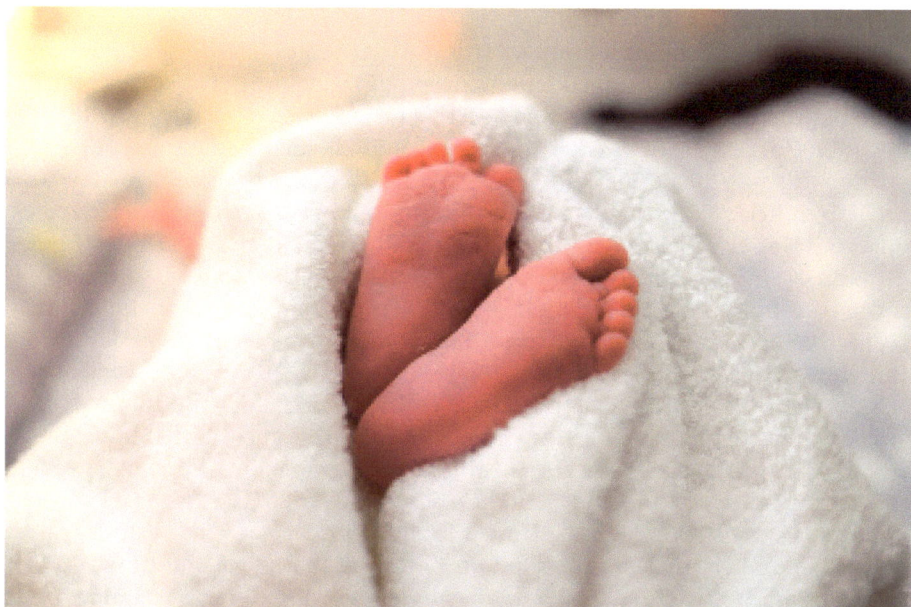

I didn't discover that I was very passive until I was about 47. By that time, I had three children (teenagers), an ex-husband, and a Master's Degree in Experimental Psychology. I had some understanding of my brand of femininity but had never characterized it as overly submissive.

Looking back, it was exactly that.

Being a girl was comfortable for me, or so I thought. It didn't matter so much that I never played with dolls and preferred board games. My family was in the toy business, and I was always allowed to select whatever I wished to play with.

I liked "boy" games better. Climbing on rocky terrain near my apartment, playing baseball in the schoolyard, and mumblety-peg on an empty lot with the boys were my choices.

I liked "girl" things, too.

My father admired me for being pretty, and I was encouraged by my mother to smile frequently to enhance my prettiness. I loved to get new clothes even though my mother picked them out until I graduated from High School. I had wonderful girlfriends and spent many hours with them after school.

But most of the girl stuff was about being a GOOD girl. A GOOD girl meant I allowed myself to be completely dominated by an authority figure, my mother. My father was not so much an authoritarian because my mother wouldn't let him. She ruled the roost. That made my father and me natural allies against her. Not so much fun for mom, I'm sure. Dad was fun to be with but powerless when it came to my protection.

My youth was like a play. My job, therefore, was to fulfill the role my mother wrote for me in her script. She directed me to suppress whatever script I tried to write for myself. She would often say, "You're not entitled to feel that way, young lady." In fact, I was not entitled to feel any way at all. Pleasant and serene were my characteristics in the play.

She told me I was too wild at my core, and I believed her.

Why else would she have been so strict? Mom positioned herself as my ally. She saved me from my so-called feral underpinnings before they became noticed by others, and I got into trouble. She described trouble as acting out my wildness. My path to success lay in passivity, quietness, and obedience to her will. I participated in this scheme because it felt safe. If asked, I would have described myself as a drab trench coat with a beautiful, colorful lining. What she characterized as dangerous was enticing to me. I was drawn to the lining of that coat.

I went off to college and graduated with a degree in Economics. Afterward, I moved back home because my mother wouldn't allow me any other choice.

Finally, it was time to get married, for me, an escape from my maladjusted family. I had lots of choices.

I was the perfect bride material: passive, pretty, energetic, and humble. And since I still believed that I needed protection from my uncontrollable nature, I selected from many proposals a man who most resembled my mother. I needed to be reined in (or so I thought), and he was the guy to do it.

Talcott Parsons worked in the United States in 1955,

He developed a nuclear family model, which at that place and time was the prevalent family structure. The Parsons model describes our household.

Education

Gender-specific education; high professional qualification is important only for the man.

Profession

The workplace is the primary area of men; career and professional advancement are deemed unimportant for women.

Housework

Housekeeping and child care are the primary functions of women; man's participation in these functions is only partially wanted.

Decision making

In case of conflict, man has the last say, for example, choosing the place to live, schools for children, buying decisions.

Child care and education

Women take care of the largest part of these functions; she educates children and cares for them in every way".

You can see how passivity fits perfectly in this framework.

My children blamed me for being passive and not defending them from their father's domination when he was on a rampage. Their accusation crushed me. My passivity almost crushed them.

Betty Friedan described in The Feminine Mystique that the female is defined by "male domination, and nurturing maternal love."

The problem was that at some point, I was no longer willing to play that game. I changed the rules, and that actually provoked my divorce. I welcomed that maybe I am untamed at heart and no longer felt that I needed any outside controller. Being passive is not me at all. I recognized that my desires matter as much as my husband's.

I think (or rather, hope) my children have forgiven me for letting them down.

I still, on occasion, fall back to my formerly passive self. But for the most part, I am free to feel what I feel, act as I wish, and select my own clothing.

IT'S CURTAINS FOR MY PIANO
Is my piano a symbol of where my life is?

Music, at its essence, is what gives us memories. And the longer a song has existed in our lives, the more memories we have of it. *Stevie Wonder*

Similarly, memories are piled on objects that have been with us for many years, especially musical instruments. My piano has been with me for 80 years. Wow! So, why not keep it? The latest scoop: no one wants it or has space for it, including me. It's a relic.

I was about nine years old when my mother decided music would be a better path for me to follow than dance. When I danced, I felt joy and freedom. Of course, music is a mandatory partner of dance, but I favored dance. Mom's question to me about learning to play the piano was really a sham; it was a decision she had already made. We had no piano, but she had hired a teacher and arranged for me to practice at Aunt Helen's apartment, nearby. Soon after I started practicing there, my parents bought me a baby grand piano to practice at home.

My first teacher was a Russian woman who believed in discipline. She kept a ruler handy to rap my knuckles if my hands fell into the incorrect position.

There was not an inkling of musicality about her method.

My next teacher was at a local music school, a young man who kept his hand in his pocket, rubbing himself constantly during my lessons. I finally told my mother that I thought he must be suffering from appendicitis, which explained his hand activity. I was about ten. It had been really creepy, and I thought if I told my mother, she would be annoyed and say, ***"Don't be ridiculous,"*** like she usually responded to my complaints. However, she acted immediately and took me out of that school. Thank goodness. Amazing how at ten years old, a girl can discern creepiness.

My piano lessons continued with a new teacher, but practicing was an issue. As I sat at the piano and practiced for a while, I would drift off into daydreaming. My mother, who was the spy in the kitchen, and who I can still hear, would scream, *"Lynn, practice!"* This scene was repeated maybe a thousand times.

I guess my effort on the piano was working since I was accepted into Music & Art High School and was enrolled at a serious music school on the upper west side of Manhattan at the same time.

The music school was in a brownstone squeezed between two massive apartment buildings on West End Avenue. In the basement of the building, there were many small teaching and practice studios. The main floor was where we had our class meetings every six weeks. At these get-togethers, every student would perform a practiced piece, which the teachers would evaluate. The students were the audience and the performers. No applause was allowed. The ambiance was funereal.

This floor-through space was paneled in mahogany, the only light coming in from the windows at the two ends of the long narrow room. Illumination came from tiny wall sconces just bright enough for the teachers to write their appraisals. Two full-size grand pianos were at the back end of the room.

It was torture.

Waiting for my turn to perform, my anxiety elevated to a hard-to-breath level. I was terrified by my anticipated performance and developed a dry cough that was unstoppable. Besides the performances, the room was absolutely silent except for the pencil scratchings of the teachers' evaluations (and my coughing). I carried cough drops with me to keep my throat moist. But they only helped sometimes.

One time, as I coughed, the lozenge in my mouth came flying out.

It landed on the floor, with a plunk, under a chair two rows in front of me. My eyes became cemented to it. There it was, a small yellow lump just sitting on the floor, almost begging me to find a way to retrieve it and get it out of sight. I imagined myself slipping down off the chair, to my knees, and then leaning forward and ducking under the chairs on which two other pupils were sitting to reach the lozenge. I couldn't do it.

Instead, I just sat there wishing somehow I would evaporate. But I didn't. The cough drop didn't evaporate either. We were trapped.

The first time the piano became my sole possession was when my husband, our baby, and I moved to Providence, R.I. There was an ideal spot for it in the living room. So we had it moved from my parent's apartment. It looked elegant, and I played it occasionally.

But, I was so busy with my son, his little brother, who arrived soon after, and then a baby sister, my playing time became less and less. I felt like I lived in an uncaged zoo with all three of them under five years old. But, it was enchanting to watch them grow and develop.

My husband got a new job in NYC, and all of us (including the piano) followed. We purchased a modest house in a suburban town with a smallish living room but one big enough for my instrument. Time went on, and we got richer and built a big luxurious house with more piano space.

Every place I lived needed to have enough space for the piano.

The kids were growing up, so they started taking piano lessons. Hearing them play inspired me to join in. I recruited their teacher to take me on as a pupil, too, and he agreed. I was shocked when he said to me after a few months of lessons, *"I'd like you to practice four hours each day, and we can arrange a small concert tour for you. You play beautifully."*

Anger flared in me instantly, betrayal. I had learned over the years to hear the music deeply. I felt its impact and beauty. Not once during my youthful years of piano study had anyone even hinted that I had any talent. Then, at that time, forty years old, I was offered a concert tour.

No way was I doing that.

Several years later, after divorcing my husband, my daughter and I moved to an apartment, of course, making sure there was room for my piano. And, then, after remarrying, moved to yet another apartment, of course, with the piano in mind.

When my granddaughter showed an interest in learning to play, I had the piano moved to my daughter's house nearby.

Here's the situation today. My daughter and family are moving to Manhattan. There will be no room for a piano. I became a widow and moved to an apartment with no room for it either. I discovered that the piano is worthless, and there is a glut of old pianos on the market that nobody wants. It's actually a burden to get rid of. The last resort would have been to chop it up and leave it out for the town to take to the dump — a truly ignoble end for an object so connected to my life; It actually hurt. Finally, we placed a post on Facebook to give it away free — and luckily, a taker has appeared.

I felt related to this instrument. If my piano is old, used-up, and unwanted, could I possibly be described in the same way; old, used up, and unwanted? Does the life of my piano mimic the thread of my life? Oh boy, I certainly hope not.

So it's goodbye piano. Thanks for everything.

I am old but still feel energetic and vital. And, I'm doing what I can to stay that way.

I am not my piano, and my piano is not me.

KISSING A HURT DOESN'T OFTEN MAKE IT BETTER
The miracle is that we can heal ourselves, sometimes.

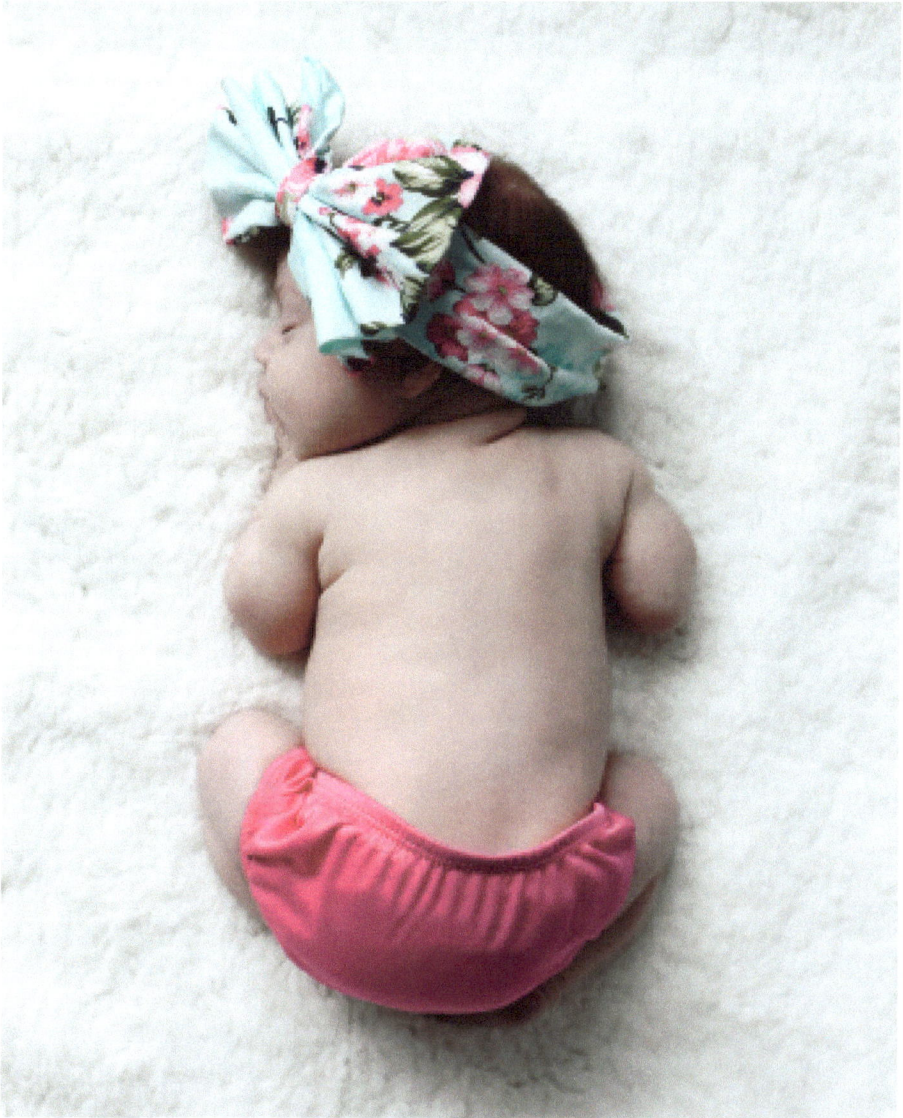

Recently, a dear friend told me, **"From here on, nothing good will happen."** We are old now, but it sounds to me like a superstitious statement rather than a forecast.

Pain can be honest, whether it's physical, emotional, or both. It certainly needs to be acknowledged and dealt with.

The statement means on the surface that aging is an unstoppable predictor of future suffering. But, it's really a different version of "Break a Leg" (in the theatrical tradition) attempting to offset fears over our ever-aging bodies and minds. It states, out loud, a wish opposite what we want to occur. It's a superstition bent on keeping pain and suffering away like a Kina Hurra, in Yiddish, to keep the evil eye away — an ancient bit of witchcraft.

What about crying, laughing, dancing, and singing to begin our Healing Arsenal?

Instead of making magical statements, we can begin to look at self-healing methods in the real world.

At sixteen years old, I go to a sailing, horse-back riding summer camp (as a camper) on Lake Champlain. When we travel to another camp for competitions, they put the horses in one truck and us in another. We all stand for the entire trip in the truck's open back and sing songs like Ninety-Nine Bottles of Beer on the Wall.

It isn't lyrical or charming singing. It's more like shouting in unison as loud as possible and, by doing that — becoming free. Not being lady-like, not being concerned about my voice quality, just singing my heart out. I look around at all my bunkmates, not giving a hoot about who hears them, and gradually, my courage grows, and I join them full force. I'm allowing the sound to burst forth from my throat without constraint.

Teenagers suffer! We all doubt the future and if we would ever evolve into at least moderately acceptable humans. But, shouting as we did into the wind, all the confusions and fears disappear. Crying and laughing can, even now, make the pain go away. These are self-healing techniques available at any age.

Modern medical developments can add to our Healing Arsenal of methodology for survival. I am afflicted with an Essential Tremor, particularly in my right hand. It has gotten so bad that I wasn't able to write. However, last week, I was lucky enough to be directed to a neurologist who treats this affliction with Botox. He was terrific, and I had my first treatment. The miracle of miracles, the therapy seems to improve my ability to control a pen, and today, I wrote a check and signed it. Hurrah! Yeah!

Neuroplasticity is another tool to add to our Healing Arsenal.

Neuroplasticity is the capacity of the brain and nervous system to renew themselves and grow new connections. Scientists knew that infants and children are born with the ability, and now, studies have shown that it functions in adults as well.

Dr. Norman Doidge is a significant contributor to these new findings. He writes that neuroplasticity represents "the most important alteration in our view of the brain since we first sketched out its basic anatomy." Also, Dr. Doidge explains we know that neuroplasticity is stimulated through precise, directed attention to a wide variety of gentle and unusual movement possibilities. The Feldenkrais Method' is the perfect vehicle for this newly discovered brain function. I've been participating in these movement classes for several years, and I feel much more in tune with my body since I started.

It's another addition to the Healing Arsenal.

According to Wikipedia, the term "neuroplasticity" was first used by Polish neuroscientist Jerzy "Konorski." In 1948, he described observed changes in neuronal structure (neurons are the cells that make up our brain). It became widely popular in the 1960s.

Another tool to add to our Healing Arsenal is Reiki.

Modern Reiki masters offer the Reiki energy to others through non-invasive gentle light pressure touch using the traditional Reiki hand positions. Reiki healing complements many medicinal therapies and conventional medicine and can assist in the potential recovery of people suffering from pain, illness, disease, and more.

And, let's not forget all the over-the-counter products available to ease pain and anxiety, and prescription drugs, too, although many of us try to use as few as possible. Nevertheless, they are helpful additions to our Healing Arsenal.

You probably remember, "Take two aspirin and call me in the morning." (the cure-all, aspirin)

In the Jewish world, the practice of Shiva, seven days of mourning after the death of a loved one, observed in ways different from ordinary daily life, is a method of self and community healing. Every religion has its observances surrounding losses. So, we can add them all to our **Healing Arsenal.**

So, here's a summary of how **good things can still happen:**

We can cry, laugh, dance, and sing.

We can use new medical discoveries, like neuroplasticity and Botox, to name a few. There are many more.

We can participate in religious rituals to ease pain arising from losses.

We can try methodologies like Feldenkrais and Reiki, which are easily found.

The potential of good things happening still exists no matter how old we are. Just as daybreak regularly appears, we can still experience healing.

MY JEWISH SURPRISES
A journey to discover my heritage.

My first surprise.

When my oldest child graduated from High School, we took a family trip to Israel. To my surprise, as the El Al plane turned toward Israel's shore and played HaTikvah over the plane's loudspeaker system, tears started streaming down my cheeks. I had no idea why.

I grew up in a family that was all about total assimilation into American culture. Our Judaism was bisected — at home, we were kosher, but we were not outside the house. We were far from Sabbath observers. My mother occasionally lit Shabbos candles, but most Friday nights, I was left home as the babysitter for my younger brother so she and my father could go to Temple.

My father took me out frequently as a little girl for lobster dinners, and each Sunday, we ate dinner at a fine downtown restaurant, none of which were kosher, as a family,

My synagogue visits were confined to the high holidays and concerned with what new outfit I would wear. Being. "too Jewish" was frowned upon, not only in my immediate family but in my extended family as well.

My second surprise

My second surprise came when my older son decided to become a Ba'al Teshuva, several years later, a returnee to the faith. I had no idea where this came from; he had certainly not been brought up to be religious. I thought he would get over it, almost like it was an affliction. However, it became clear that this was his permanent choice, so radically different from my lifestyle.

I felt isolated and abandoned by him. My next child, another son, had no such leanings.

This is my third surprise.

My daughter (third child) decided to live a more Jewish life. She enrolled as a Melton student. She graduated two years later and went on to become a Bat Mitzvah after that. I'm very proud of her as I am of my two sons.

The Florence Melton Mini-School offers adults who did not have the opportunity to learn Jewish tradition and history as children. It's a two-year program.

I toyed with the idea of enrolling as a Melton student myself but did nothing about it until a few more years had passed. At that time, my life felt particularly empty. I was focusing on what I might do to enrich my existence.

My fourth surprise.

My fourth surprise came about when I awoke one morning during this period with the clear decision to enroll in the Melton mini-school. So I did just that. It was a part of my life that I owned, a birthright, that I was entitled to delve into. For thousands of years, my family has been and still is Jewish.

The two years I spent there were exactly what I had been hoping for regarding my heritage. I learned many things about Jewish history and practices and learned how little I actually knew when I started.

Here's what I learned about the structure of prayers:

This structure is common, and my description is meant to be taken light-heartedly. Part one is about praise. God, you are great, you are wonderful, all-powerful, there is no one like you and never will be. Part two, plead your case. It could be somewhat like this: God, if you have time or a minute to spare, I need a little help. I know I'm not worth your effort, but could you please help me out with this problem. Then, name the problem. Part three, thank God for listening, being helpful to you, even though you are unworthy. It's a return to praise.

My Lack of knowledge came as no surprise.

My journey towards Judaism may have started with Ha Tikvah on the plane to Israel, but I knew it wouldn't end there.

This all took place about 10 years ago, during which time I took various post-Melton courses but not too much recently. In the face of the COVID-19, this may be the perfect time to continue my journey.

MY MOTHER
A story of jealousy, talent, and forgiveness.

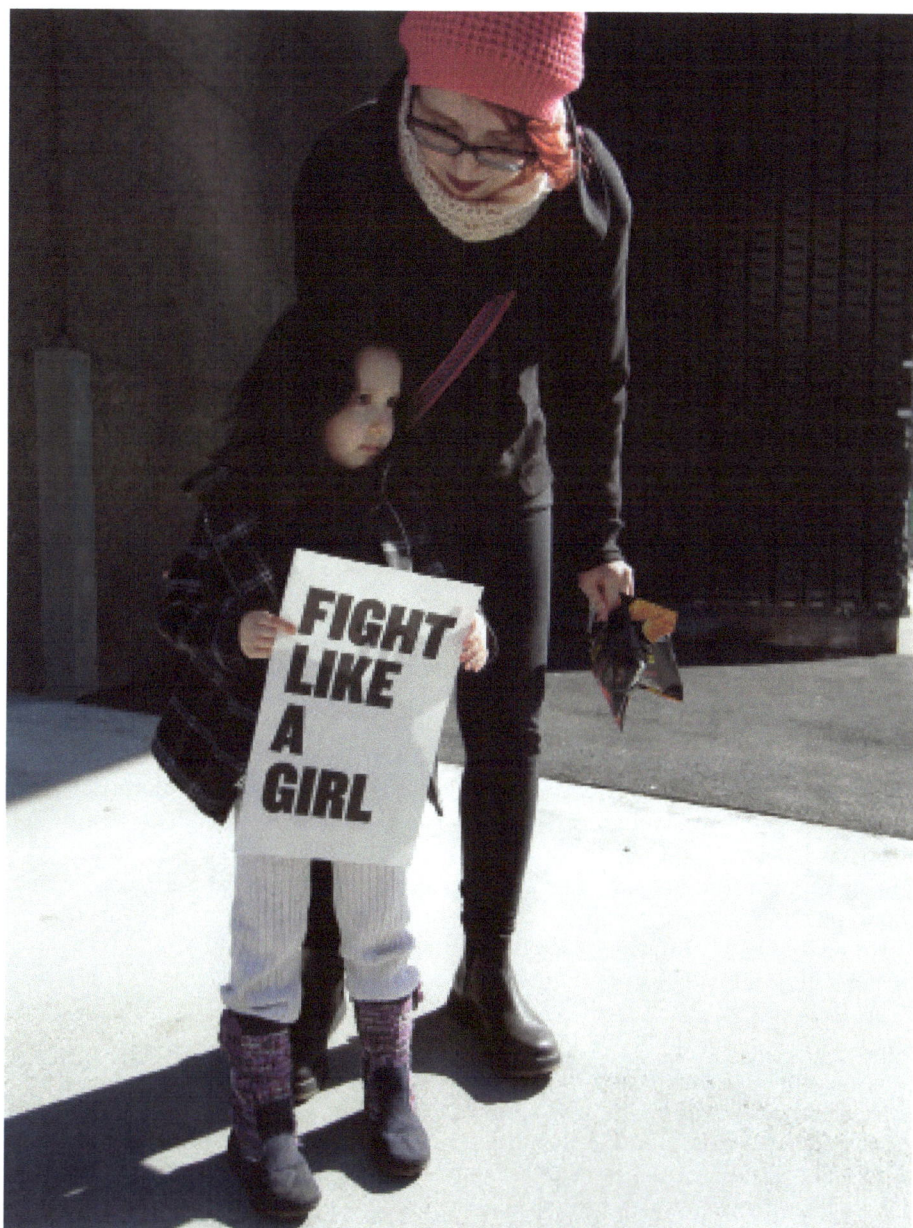

My mother was ninety and hospitalized for Congestive Heart Failure when I came to visit her. She decided to compare our hands. "Let me see your hands," she says. And I do. She then places her hand next to mine and says, "My hands look younger than yours." She was right. Her hands did look younger; she cared about the comparison and was gratified that she had bested me. She had a need to point out our differences, with her coming out on top.

Everyone knew that my mother was the smartest person in the room. No matter the topic, she had a full grasp of it and was only too happy to tell you that her information was the gospel truth. There was no need to look for another's version. She didn't make a lot of friends while expounding her knowledge on one subject or another.

She was formidable.

My mother was a devotee of the Victorian Age and its sensibilities. She must have decided it was proper to act in a lady-like fashion: demure, modest, and even mousy. And, in her interpretation of the tenets of Victorianism, one never discussed feelings.

At all costs, feelings had to be suppressed.

This attitude probably came from novels and magazines she read. Certainly, her background and upbringing didn't warrant it. She grew up in a small town in northeastern Pennsylvania's coal country and lived in a house that served as both a dry goods store (from which the family made a living) on the main level and lived on the upper floors. She was the second girl of five siblings, the three youngest being boys.

The family moved to the Bronx when her older sister approached marriageable age for fear that she might marry out of the Jewish faith. There were just five other Jewish families in that little town. My mother was about thirteen when they moved.

My grandfather and all the children were obsessed with cars, the world's newest toys. Grandpa knew that cars needed a place to be stored when not in use. So he opened the very first garage in the East Bronx. Not only did he house the cars, but his boys and my mother could also repair them. She pointed out that she had learned to drive backwards before driving forward from her experience parking cars in their garage. Sometimes, she told me, she parked so close to another car she had to climb out through the window.

We had rented a bungalow in the country one summer, and my father was coming up for the weekend when a disaster happened. We had a flat tire on our way to pick him up at the train.

No problem! My mother changed the flat tire all by herself.
I watched her with amazement.

She was multi-talented. She cooked mouthwatering food and was a creative seamstress. She sewed much of my clothing throughout my childhood, and designed and stitched gorgeous gowns for me to wear for formal events in my college years, always urging me to cover up more of my body than I wanted to, i.e., my arms and shoulders. She painted, too, delicate Japanese Ink artworks, as well as oils. She was a genius at solving crossword puzzles.

My father's business moved from one location to another, and my mother created a mechanical drawing to facilitate the move. It was precise down to the last 1/4".

She was a master at everything — a renaissance woman, born before her time.
For the first seven years of my life, I was the only child until my brother was born. During those years, my mother came up with a model for my development into which I had to squeeze myself. She set out to create the perfectly trained girl

child, well-bred, adhering to her rules, very Victorian. I was that child. These rules were fundamental to her. Maybe she thought of me as the "tabula rasa," an empty vessel that she could fill with her knowledge of how to stay alive in a dangerous world.

My father was a prosperous businessman and loved the "good life." He wore what mattered to him, and since he was handsome, with piercing blue eyes, he often wore navy blue suits to enhance his eye color. He was a good dancer, told funny jokes, enjoyed good food in upscale restaurants, and tried to be my protector when I needed it from my mother's strictness. He taught me songs from his days in the U.S. Navy, not necessarily appropriate for a little girl to sing. But to me, everything he did was so much fun; I treasured my time with him.

And he treasured his time with me. He thought I was the prettiest, smartest girl ever created and showed me off to his friends whenever he could. Often dad didn't include my mother on these outings. You can imagine how that must have made her feel.

Finally, as an adult, I realized she had become very jealous of my father's attention to me. I thought she was always mad at me because I was disobedient. So I tried harder and harder to be upstanding and do things the right way. I desperately wanted to please her, but nothing I did seemed good enough. I always felt she might have loved me, but she didn't like me very much.

I know now that my behavior was not the underlying issue.

I remember her speaking with her confidants on the phone after I had done something that displeased her. She would say, speaking about me, "She's not going to get away with that." I heard that particular phrase often. It was said with war-like vigor.

And, I didn't get away with anything! Ever! My mother was smothering me. I felt buried alive.

Getting away with simple "stuff" is good for a child's sense of self-reliance and autonomy. My mother left me no space for either. It became all about her and how well she brought me up. I felt like my job was to stand behind her quietly until such time she wanted me to perform, either on the piano or to dance. Then, back to my position behind her.

During these years, I was not aware of her multiple miscarriages. She and my father must have become sadder and sadder about not being able to complete a pregnancy. Finally, they produced a son who seemed perfect but turned out to have significant emotional deficits, limited contact with reality, and was a heartbreak from the get-go.

He still is today. His condition was a disaster for my parents, not one they had ever bargained for. Their disappointment about him never went away. So, they decided to raise him as if he was normal. He dominated our family life which became anything but normal. They sought diagnoses from doctors but wouldn't accept anything the doctors said. That's how mental illness was dealt with in those days.

It became a catastrophe for me, too, not knowing I was soon to become his caregiver. I love him and still take care of him both emotionally and financially. I do everything I can to make his life better, but he is demanding and very paranoid.

My first child came along, a perfect boy, and my mother bonded with him immediately. Circumstances caused us to move apart, we to Providence R.I. and they to Sullivan County, NY.

She helped us move to Providence, and when it came time for her to leave, she said, looking at my son, "I can't bear to leave him." She said nothing to me. It was the first time I ever heard her say anything about her feelings. "I love you" had no place in her vocabulary to anyone, certainly not to me. She was stoic, but I felt deserted and unloved when she didn't acknowledge she was leaving me too. Maybe her jealousy of me extended to my having a well-child, while she didn't.

I had decided that I wanted to tell my mother I loved her during her hospitalization. It was the first time I would verbalize the word "love" between us. So, I faced up to this giant, my mother, and told her, "I love you." It came out in a whisper. She looked stunned and said nothing. I hastily said goodbye, ran out of the room, hoping to make it to my car before the flood of my tears started flowing.

This is a story that has been brewing in me for a long time. I needed to write it.

NEEDING HELP IS HARD TO ADMIT
We are examining the reasons why.

What exactly is a need?

In an article, "Doyal and Gough's Intermediate Needs." on changingminds. org, there is a list of needs for physical health and personal autonomy. They are: food and water, protective housing, a safe work environment, clothing, safety, appropriate health care, security in childhood, meaningful primary relations with others, economic security, safe birth control, and child-bearing.

I'm focusing on "meaningful primary relations with others" (like my mother) and "security in childhood." (received from my mother, father, and teachers.)

Mom taught me that I had to rely on myself because nobody else would help me. She conveyed this lesson by not showing up when I needed her, or if she did appear, siding with my opponents. Dad was fun to be with but was busy working, so his contribution toward "childhood security" was money. Some teachers were more into their own neuroses than worrying about offering security to their students.

I'm in third-grade elementary school, and we move to a new apartment. This means changing schools, too. Our new place is across the street from the school, so I can see my apartment building if I look out the school windows.

It makes me feel safe.

Mom drops me off at school, and I watch the back of her walking down the school's front steps, feeling lost. She doesn't turn back and wave at me. I'm alone but mostly nervous. I don't know anyone or even where the girl's room is. I'm escorted to my classroom and presented to my teacher, Mrs. Steiger, whom I later silently rename "Mrs. Tiger."

The morning sessions are peaceful. We learn long division, which turns out more accessible than I thought it would be. I was worried about the long division.

The atmosphere in my classroom is different after lunch. For some unknown reason, Mrs. Steiger becomes Mrs. Tiger as she starts yelling non-stop at the boys in my class. Every afternoon session, she yells at them and sometimes calls one of them up to the front of the classroom to administer a stronger face-to-face shout. She grabs any particularly troublesome boy by his shirt collar and throws him against the blackboard. The boys don't even cry. I would. The rest of the room is silent, staring, as we watch this frightening scene.

It's like this every day, and I don't complain about these horrendous afternoon hours to my mother since I know she won't do anything. According to her, the teacher is right all the time. It is the current zeitgeist.

Sonna, my classmate, puts her head on her desk as the onslaught continues. Mrs. "Tiger," asks what's wrong. Sonna says she has a headache, so she's sent to the nurse. Lucky her, she's out of the screeching and head-banging for the remainder of the day. The next day, she does the same thing and gets the same result. She goes to the Nurse's room.

I am so upset by these episodes; I'm desperate to escape. So, I try the Sonna technique. And, it works! I put my head on the desk and complained of a head-ache. Out I go to the nurse, where I remain until the day ends. Certainly, I don't tell Mom.

Of course, there is a problem, a big problem. I really don't have a headache; I am lying. I complained again the following day. However, this time I'm sent to the Principal's office rather than to the nurse. It's called "being busted." The Principal and the school nurse are there, and after a few minutes, my mother arrives. Oh, no!

No one asks me how I feel or why I have created this fake headache. Instead, the Principal asks my mother, "Do you know of any reason why Lynn should have repeating headaches?"

"No, absolutely not," she says immediately and adds, "She is fine," further breaking faith with me.

My disappointment over her response is profound. Without losing a minute, she answers and substantiated my offense; lying. Why didn't she, before answering, asked me what was going on and why I had made up this story. I knew the reason, immediately. My feelings never matter; what matters is her embarrass-ment by my behavior, how it reflects on her mothering, and that fix comes first. I must be a worthless liar in her mind. I realize she is more important to me than I am to her, and I can't count on her being on my side or standing up for me.

So, here was my "meaningful primary relation," sacrificing me to stand with the other grown-ups in the room, throwing me under the bus so she could regain her respectability.

This episode smashes my self-esteem. I feel mortified, worthless. Maybe I could crawl into my own skin and vanish. I vow that I will totally rely on myself to solve any obstacles in the future. Expect only the worst from others. Avoiding a re-occurrence is paramount, so keeping my problems to myself is the path to follow since my most treasured protector, my mother, has forsaken me and I must be my own champion.

Returning to my classroom is a further humiliation. Everyone will know that I was caught in a lie. While walking back to my desk, I stare at the floor, too embarrassed to make eye contact, even with my friends.

It's a good thing that the secret garden I created in my head always has its gates open.

It amazes me that this one incident has had so much impact on my life. I learned that resolving my own issues without anyone knowing they exist avoids a recurrence of my being disgraced. My exterior becomes smooth regardless of my interior. I act as if nothing is ever troubling me.

Now, later in life, I'm different. I found my voice and use it when needed. I have found trustworthy people, I've given birth to them, and I'm grateful for their love, caring, and support. I have sweet, kind friends, and I'm open to give and take relationships. I value receiving their assistance when I need it.

ONE LETTER CONNECTS "MOTION" AND "EMOTION"
How can adding a little letter lead us to realize a new connection?

I've offered a list of values that was comprehensive and a little bit overwhelming. How could we possibly deal with so many of them at one time? So, this week, let's look at one of them. Let's examine "vitality."

To be sure we are on the same page, here's a definition of the word: the state of being fit and active; energy.

There are all kinds of ways to fill your life with vitality. My all-time favorite is dance. (More about that later). When I think about the word, however, I remember climbing. Not these days, of course — I can hardly climb onto a step stool now. As a kid, I lived in a hilly area, and much of it was in its natural state, filled with trees, low shrubbery, and boulders. Every day, after school, my friend, Candy, and I would climb up and down the hills, romping across the terrain with ease and grace. It made me feel vigorous and muscly.

Add an "e" to the word "motion," and the resulting "emotion" can often describe joy.

(My mother wasn't so happy about this activity because I returned home for dinner very dirty. As I washed my hands before we ate, and the water splashed onto my forearms, it left rivulets of clean skin peeking out from under all the rest of the grime on my arms. I loved how it looked.)

I started dancing just about before I could walk or soon after. My mother told of my spontaneous dancing whenever there was music. Dance lessons began when I was three years old and continued until I was about 17. At one time, I danced "on point" and also learned to tap dance. There were many dance recitals in beautiful costumes, which my mother made. She also made the costumes for the rest of the neighborhood girls whose mothers couldn't sew. I was proud of her.

My recitals were exhilarating but not too much fun.

The vitality which recitals provided was palpable, but I don't remember those times as bringing happiness. Mostly, my feelings were anxiety about making a mistake or worrying that I looked too fat.

Later, I studied dance with Hanya Holm, one of the four creators of Modern Dance.

Hanya Holm, a developer of the modern dance movement, who choreographed Kiss Me, Kate, My Fair Lady and Camelot was my teacher during my high school years. Her dance style stressed the importance of exploring floor patterns and spatial dimensions and remained based on universal physical principles for motion. Her style was both physical and intellectual. In one session we were asked to locate our center of gravity. Then we imagined it had moved out of our bodies to the space alongside us but about three feet away. The class members tilted toward their centers. Then we walked across the studio in a slalom-like path shifting our gravity from one side to the other. It resulted in a lovely semicircular pattern of movement. Her improvisational style spoke to me!

Dancing joyously came to me naturally.

My dear cousin, now gone, and I would frequently get together to dance in her apartment. We would listen to Liszt's Hungarian Rhapsodies and move. These were marvelous unsupervised times. Neither of us commented on what the other was doing. The movements came from our interior places of youthful vitality, repressed joy, and often, secret places of pain.

The connection between "motion" and "emotion" was apparent.

Dancing is extraordinary, even now, as I become older. For me, moving through space, either in a rehearsed way or not, even in my kitchen, creates freedom. I can see that perhaps a roller-coaster ride might duplicate this feeling. Many folks, including my granddaughter, love wild rides at a carnival. It's only after writing this that I can see the connection. Carnival rides also create freedom. Breezes rushing across your cheeks and your body speeding upward and then down again are seductive, urging you to find them again. They move you away from yesterday and tomorrow, leaving you only with now.

I examined the meaning and structure of the words.

I'm intrigued that it has taken me so long to connect "motion" and "emotion." I looked up the two words and found that they have the same Latin root, MOTUS. No wonder these words together teach us something about where to find "vitality" and "happiness." Maybe when people talk about the Life Force, they are talking about this connection.

Think about how you seek and find your "vitality." How does "motion" morph into "emotion" for you? How does realizing this connection enhance your life?

SKIN-TO-SKIN CONTACT, OVER FOR NOW!
How I feel about being quarantined.

It occurred to me that I have not touched (nor have I been touched by anyone) in about 8 weeks. Can you imagine taking this long to notice? The strange thing is that it really doesn't seem to matter to me — maybe!

As I explained before, being alone doesn't seem to matter to me either. So who would have thought that a pandemic helped me to discover that I could basically live as a hermit? Maybe I should have been an astronaut and lived alone in a space capsule!

Touching has so many meanings. The touch of my husband's arms around me before we went to sleep made me feel safe. It reminded me why, as a young child I felt afraid. It was the long-forgotten memories of childhood monsters that used to live in my closet.

Growing up, I couldn't sleep with my closet doors open. What if the monsters came out during the night and kidnapped me? I was so scared. I would be ok with the doors closed and my long hair tucked under the covers. That way, they wouldn't know that I was a girl. I was sure girls got kidnapped, not boys. I think my husband's arms around me allowed me to remember them and finally dump them.

Touches can be gentle and loving. I remember lovingly touching my children, but what if my memory is false? I don't remember ever being touched myself as a child. So what if I thought I touched them, but didn't?

I hope that's not true.

Touching is also a vital part of intimacy. In sex therapy, one touches one's partner all over. Not intercourse, just touching. The intercourse comes later on.

A wonderful article was written in the September 2010 Greater Good Magazine, which is based at UC Berkeley, by Dacher Kettner Ph.D., professor of Psychology at UC Berkeley. It is called Hands-On Research: The Science of Touch. This comprehensive article outlines much of the scientific studies published around the same time. They show the importance and benefits humans can derive from touching.

It was Descartes, however, in the early 1600s that pushed the western world to trust reason instead of physical contact to gain knowledge. His ideas still dominate our culture. In other parts of the world, touching is more acceptable.

In today's world, struck by the Corona Virus, touching is specifically prohibited and downright dangerous unless it is part of family life. Living alone, as I do, eliminates touching. I fully understand the need for not touching, but it is lonely and feels isolating.

I am confined to myself as if an invisible cloak surrounds me. Harry Potter used his invisibility cloak to assist him in his adventures. My cloak ensures my separation from other people.

Humans touching each other is a necessary and natural part of our life's experience.

It calms a deep inner place in our nervous systems. So, living alone without skin-to-skin contact during this quarantine is particularly difficult.

Hugging is another wonderful experience, also missing from my life. And when you come right down to it, touching during handshakes is also wonderful as it contains elements of trust, warmth, and acceptance. I wonder if this behavior will ever be a normal activity again. I wonder what normal will actually look like after a vaccine is developed.

I wonder if I'll ever get to touch someone again.

SOMETIMES THE COW DOES JUMP OVER THE MOON
What it's like to experience out-of-body events.

Did you ever experience your body as being in two places at the same time? Have you ever experienced overwhelming joy brought on by visual and auditory stimulation?

Surprisingly, when I looked up Out-of-Body (OBE) experiences on Wikipedia, I found a ton of material. Here are a few excerpts:

The term out-of-body experience was introduced in 1943 by G. N. M. Tyrrell in his book Apparitions, G. N. M. Tyrrell, Apparitions, Gerald Duckworth and Co. Ltd, London, 1943, pp. 149.

Scientists consider the OBE to be an experience from a mental state, like a dream or an altered state of consciousness without recourse to the paranormal Blackmore, Susan. (2002). Out-of-Body Experiences. Pp. 164–169. In Michael Shermer. The Skeptic Encyclopedia of Pseudoscience. ABC-CLIO. ISBN 978–1576076538.

One in ten people have an OBE once, or more commonly, several times in their life. Journal of Parapsychology, Vol. 48, September 1984 A PSYCHOLOGICAL THEORY OF THE OUT-OF-BODY EXPERIENCE by Susan Blackmore

So, here's what happened to me:

I am lucky enough to be invited to a concert at Carnegie Hall and fortunate to be seated in a first-level box directly in the center of that marvelous acoustical space. And, I'm sitting in the front chair of the box. There are people on either side of me, but that doesn't matter. What matters is that there is no one in front of me, blocking my view.

It's me and the Munich Philharmonic's performance on April 3, 2017, and, more importantly, the emptiness, nothing but space between me and the orchestra.

It's as if this space is on stand-by, ready to swell its sound to me and me alone. The music starts, and it is divine.

During the performance of Maurice Ravel's Piano Concerto in G Major, I closed my eyes.

As I sit there, I feel myself (and my chair) traveling upward and moving into the nothingness above the orchestra seats. I am suspended in the air.

I know if I open my eyes, I will find myself right back sitting in the box. But as I keep my eyes closed I can see myself levitating. The feeling is glorious and privileged as I am suspended alone. There is nothing but emptiness on each side, above, below, or behind me, and the whole orchestra in front of me. The music has taken control and absorbed me and my chair as we hover. We have fused. This is a spectacular feeling, and I almost giggle out loud to myself as I relish where I am.

Then I open my eyes and, as expected, me (and my chair) are still in the box. So, I dare to do it again. I close my eyes and successfully travel in my mind's eye into the now comfortable space, which has become my private property, suspended alone.

What a rush that was!

I've had other exultations of spirit during my life, but nothing as dramatic. While driving as a ten-year-old with my family one early morning, we pass by a field of tall grass as the sun rises behind it, casting an anticipatory golden glow through the spaces between the blades and above them, like a halo preparing to take over the awaiting sky. The sun is on the cusp of showing itself, and I am filled with wonder. My breath quickened from happiness. The beauty of this scene surpasses anything I have ever seen before.

I am afraid to tell anyone afterward because it means exposing an intimate feeling. To me, this feels dangerous. So, I treasure this secret moment.

Agnes DeMille's choreography in the original "Oklahoma" has the dancers flowing from either side of the stage, weaving patterns of motion; I gasp at its complexity and energy. Some of the dancers walked forward and some backward, always melting into newer patterns. Seeing the interweaving of the dancers around and through each other is dazzling to watch. I am frozen in those moments. I am about 13 years old at the time.

Similarly, some 15 years later, I stood up and cheered at the end of Judith Jamison's powerful performance of the ballet "Cry" from Alvin Ailey Dance Theater. The work and choreography embody truth, grace, and strength.

In Positive Psychology, a flow state, also known colloquially as being in the zone, probably describes my state of being during these memorable experiences. The psychologist Mihaly Csíkszentmihályi described a person in a flow state as one who performs or watches an activity, fully immersed in a feeling of energized focus, full involvement, and enjoyment in the action of the event. You may wish to look for Flow: The Psychology of Optimal Experience, a Csíkszentmihályi outline of his theory. He was recognized with various awards during the years 2009-2014 and is still working. In essence, flow is the complete absorption in what one does and a resulting transformation in one's sense of time.

I will be watching for my next zone or OBE event. I hope I don't have to wait too long.

THE EVOLUTION OF A SCAREDY-CAT
Here is my journey from timidity to confidence.

My earliest memories are about how I saved myself from destruction. I used to be afraid of the man-in-the-moon, witches in my closet, dogs, cats, mice, and creepy crawlers, over which I had no control. To say I acknowledged my vulnerability would have been an understatement. I was a willing partner.

For example, my parents sent me to sleep away camp when I was seven, the summer my brother was born. It was my habit to awaken at about 5:00 AM to go to the bathroom. My slippers made a clopping sound and awakened my counselor each morning, and so she told me I was not allowed to get out of bed until 7:00. Without any objection from me, I laid in bed and "held it in" until the counselor awoke. Bravely, on visiting day, I told my grandmother, and she bought me a pair of silent slippers. The thought of my grandmother reprimanding the counselor about her poor judgment frightened me, so I pleaded with her not to say anything. I was dreading the counselor's retaliation against me, which would leave me, once again, too vulnerable to tolerate.

"Making Up" was how I gained control.

I couldn't tolerate having anyone angry with me. Introspection (and therapy) led me to understand that my "making-up" behavior was a survival technique and protection against being hurt physically or emotionally. Also, making up with the person I imagined was angry with me gave me control of the relationship in which, otherwise, I had none.

This behavior went on for years and years. My friends thought of me as easy-going, calm, and adaptable. Completely hidden was my desperate desire to avoid being hurt or abandoned and my desire to be loved.

It was my divorce that turned the tide.

I was married to my first husband for 20 years, and he was the boss of everything. I couldn't stand it. He owned it all: the money, our children, the houses we lived in, our friends, even the contents of my pocketbook. The area he couldn't control was his bad relationships at his workplace, resulting in his being a habitual job loser. He was very paranoid and physically massive, a bully, and an alcoholic. When I told him I wanted a divorce, he threatened to kill me. I was petrified and had all I could do to survive. He was my worst nightmare. For him, on the other hand, my passivity, my agreeableness made me his perfect wife. So, he fought against the divorce like a tiger.

I had the assistance of a powerful lawyer, who debunked most of his physical and financial threats against our children and me. After two and a half years of misery, my divorce was finalized. I had not only survived but felt free and liberated. I was scared but happy, with a full range of emotions. The realization of having accomplished the daunting task of legally separating from him filled me with confidence I lacked.

My next big breakthrough was years later, during my training to become a life coach.

I had just retired from my successful corporate job and decided to become a life coach. Part of the training was to learn about ourselves. In that way, we would identify what our clients were saying without accidentally interjecting what had more to do with us than with them.

In one lesson, we unpacked self-destructive behavior and identified "gremlins," those innermost negative thoughts that controlled us. Gremlins tell us what not to do. They blame everything on our insufficiencies, like being too dumb, or too short, or too ugly. They tell us, for example, that we are not good enough or smart enough to answer a question in class because our answers will be wrong and shame us.

But, gremlins also protect us from harm, or embarrassment, or doing foolhardy things. Giving them up can feel like losing our greatest guardians. I volunteered as the subject of the class exercise and agreed to give up my "gremlins."

This exercise started with a conversation with the leader about what giving up gremlins might mean to me. A chalk line was then drawn on the floor and once I stepped over it, my gremlins would be gone. I felt so afraid to do this I was crying. It was a powerful moment in my life. Freeing myself from my fear of being noticed, stepping forward and abandoning my excuses for mediocrity was terrifying. As I stepped over the line, I morphed into a different person, and I was able to abandon my ancient need to hide. All my classmates cried with me over my new freedom and the teachers, too.

So, I am no longer a scaredy-cat. It took long enough!

Since then, my life has changed. I still go out of my way to avoid friction with anyone for fear they will abandon me. But, if it happens, I am not afraid. Now, sometimes, people make up with me. I'm worth the effort.

58

THE FUNERAL OF MY PAINTED TURTLES
How I learned that death is part of living.

Painted turtles were thought of as toys for kids to play with. Artists took these live, tiny creatures and painted lovely designs on their shells. You could buy a bunch of them at a time and watch them crawl over and under each other for fun. Now, of course, we realize they were tortured. I feel regretful about their treatment.

It was the summer of 1942, and my family and my cousin's family rented a two-family house in Far Rockaway that was about two blocks from the beach. We had the second-floor apartment and aunt, uncle, and cousins, the first. We shared caring for and watching our newest toys, painted turtles.

The first thing we did every day after breakfast was to check on them. Well, you can guess, one lovely summery morning, we found that they had all died.

It was so disappointing. My cousin and I loved them.

(More about the funeral in a moment.)

I was not a stranger to death, however. Until I was about five years old, my grandfather (my dad's father) lived with us. He was very jolly and very Orthodox. He never put a razor to his face to shave his beard since the Torah forbids it. In preparation for Shabbat each week, however, he used a depilatory for hair removal. It had a nasty smell that permeated our entire apartment. My mother complained bitterly about the odor to my father every week. It was scary to listen to what they said to each other.

Grandpa also made his own wine in our apartment. He would get a big metal tub and lots of grapes he washed and then placed them into the tub. Then he would remove his shoes and socks, roll up his pant's legs, wash his feet and step right into the tub to stomp around on the grapes to crush them. I was finally old enough to join him in the stomping. He made it so much fun; we sang songs together in the process.

One day when I was about five, men came to our apartment and went into his room. They had a wicker stretcher with them. After a few minutes, they came out wheeling something I knew was my grandfather's remains. A matching wicker lid covered him, his face too. It looked like a mummy case to me. I knew he had died, and when I asked my mother where they were taking him, she said," He's going to Florida for a vacation."

I knew she was trying to protect me by lying, so I let the lie pass because I was afraid.

Several years later, walking with my mother as we crossed the Grand Concourse in the Bronx, I told her I knew Grandpa had died. She was shocked, and she asked me how I knew this. I actually didn't know how I knew; I just felt his death in every inch of my being. She never noticed that I had never asked about him after he was gone.

My next confrontation with death came to my other Grandpa (my mother's father.) Five years had passed, and we were at the wedding of my youngest uncle. The reception after the ceremony was like happiness, doubled, lots of dancing and fun. Grandpa had danced and danced. He was so gladdened by this wedding as this was the last of his children to be married. He and my grandma were going on a trip.

We were waiting in the lobby for the cars to take us home. I was standing in the circle of relatives when suddenly, my grandpa leaned to the side and then fell onto the floor. "Jake, Jake, what's the matter?" my grandma screamed. No answer, of course. My grandpa Jake had died there, at his son's wedding.

My mother instantly bustled my cousins and me into another room where the wedding venue had stored extra chairs. It was separated from the main waiting room by a black velvet curtain. My Mom instructed us not to peek out from behind the curtain, but of course, we did. Everyone was crying. My middle uncle, the doctor, came and started mouth-to-mouth resuscitation on my grandpa.

Mom's reaction typified how children were dealt with in those years when confronted with such losses. I later learned that she was, herself, terrified of death. Maybe other families did it differently. Hiding the children was my family's style.

So, back to our painted turtles' funeral.

No one quite knew what to do with these dead turtles. Flushing them down the toilet would certainly clog it. Throwing them in the garbage would not be thoughtful enough to assuage our loss, my cousin's and mine.

Luckily, my grandma (Mom's mom) came to visit us on that day. She had the perfect solution. She got a box of kleenex and carefully wrapped each dead turtle in its own kleenex shroud, and laid them side-by-side in a box. There were sixteen of them. Then we had a processional consisting of my grandma, my cousin, and me, down the street to the nearest sewer opening. Slowly she threw each little shroud containing turtle into the sewer, the three of us saying goodbye to each one as the sewer accepted them. It was over. Grandma was the best fixer!

Then we went to the beach to play in the sand and surf.

My grandma was very sick with cancer, and my mother would not allow me to see her before she died to say goodbye. She didn't want me to be left with sorrowful memories of how she looked at the end. I was at home when it happened, and my father came home to tell me. I immediately started to cry, but he warned me not to let my mother see me crying. He said, "Your mother feels bad enough. Seeing you crying will make it worse for her." So I didn't. I cried alone.

Denying death's permanence doesn't make it go away. It makes mourning a very solitary event and leaves an isolated mourner to understand that their feelings don't matter. It is a complicated situation. I felt so much sadness and loss yet wasn't allowed to share those intense feelings. It was more important to protect Mom. I was ten at that time.

Ironically, I'm writing this on New Year's Eve. I am looking forward to the good things I hope are coming next year, but I seem to be focused on losses here. Maybe years end and dying are two sides of the same coin.

My best wishes for a happy and healthy New Year.

WAIT, WAIT! IT'S ONLY A FEW EXTRA POUNDS
My lifetime of struggles being overweight.

It's the food.

I love food, all kinds, like soft and creamy, hard and chewy, spicy or sweet, hot or cold. I started eating olives when I was two years old. I guess I was born with a spicy palette. Chinese food is still a delicious event to me but so is American, French, Italian — you name it. I still look forward to the next meal.

And I delight in good food, not slap-dash any old thing — fresh ingredients, prepared thoughtfully, and served with panache. My dad also loved good food served with elegance, so, with my palette and his elegance, I was destined to have a weight problem.

My father grew up on the lower East Side of Manhattan, and my family frequently visited that area.

When we passed Katz's Deli, my father didn't just pass it.

We'd stopped in for a "quicky" hot dog on a bun with sauerkraut. My mother always scolded him for overfeeding me, but it was his way of showing me love and fun. Or, if we went for a walk in the park on a Sunday afternoon, he made sure it was always accompanied by an ice cream cone, double scoop.

Food, fun, and love went together.

One day, when I was about thirteen years old, I noticed my shadow on the sidewalk. I was shocked to observe I had breasts and a butt. Wow! To say I was thrilled by this development would have been an understatement.

I was becoming a woman.

As I walked home, I saw my mother with my uncle watching me as I approached them, whispering to each other. He was my favorite uncle. I felt they were talking about how I looked. I even thought they were about to compliment my new shape. I was euphoric, but no one knew or cared about how I felt.

Instead, my mother said, "Your uncle thinks you put on a lot of weight, and you look fat." My heart sank. With that statement, he'd crushed my delight in this new body. I felt guilty about my joy and was instantly revolted by how I looked.

My mother had already been at war with me because of my weight, and his remark augmented her disgust and embarrassment with my eating behavior.

By then, I was in High School, and lunch was available at the cafeteria, but my mother decided she would make my lunch to assist in my weight loss effort. The lunch consisted of a few celery sticks filled with a teaspoon of cottage cheese, some carrot sticks, and cucumber stalks. I ask you, "Is this an appropriate lunch for a growing girl"? The answer is no, and by the end of the school day, I was famished.

I got a small allowance, and I used it to buy a tuna fish sandwich and a black and white ice cream soda every day on my way home. Of course, I never mentioned that to Mom.

One day, when I arrived home, my mother told me that our neighbor had seen me at the Hilltop pharmacy, the site of my afterschool snacks. She asked what I was doing there, and the neighbor told her I was eating at the luncheonette counter in the pharmacy.

In other words, I was busted.

Hell hath no fury like my mother's. She accused me of not caring about all her efforts on my behalf and vowed she would never waste her time making lunch for me again. And she didn't.

I was secretly relieved because I didn't have to eat all that "rabbit food." I could eat normal lunches that didn't advertise my overweight condition. Truthfully, I wasn't all that overweight. It was about 20 lbs. But the extra pounds made me look matronly at 16.

During my first year away at college, instead of gaining the Freshman 25, I lost it. When my mother came to pick me up at Penn Station, she didn't recognize me and walked right on by. I was shocked and had to call her to stop.

By the time I was married and had my third child, my OB/GYN told me I needed to lose weight.

He did this by forcefully removing the sheet covering my naked body on the examining table and slowly eyed me up and down, humiliating me to the max.

He said if I were not thinner, my husband would lose interest in me and seek out the company of one of the nurses at the hospital where he worked. He was an MD.

So, I joined Weight Watchers (now WW) and lost 25 pounds. By New Year's Eve, I was very trim. I found myself surrounded at a party by all my friend's husbands, eager to impress me. This was not what I had in mind.

So, with gusto, I gained the weight back, and life returned to normal.

Ironically today, I am obliged to weigh and measure every morsel of food I put in my mouth. As I've mentioned in prior articles, I became a Type 1 Diabetic at about 60 and then lost forty pounds without even trying. To keep my blood glucose levels in a reasonable range, I must evaluate all my food.

Life's developments are freakish. My last job was working for WW for 16 years, first as a meeting leader and then as a receptionist (the weigh-in person). Part of my qualifications for this job were my own lifetime weight loss issues. Also, I was a life/time WW member, meaning I had attained my goal weight.

So, if you're struggling with weight loss issues, I am sad for you. Remember, only 12-year-old athletic boys can usually eat whatever and whenever they choose, without gaining extra pounds. Dealing with a lifetime's over-eating habits is gritty. These habits are so hard to give up. Have courage and perseverance. Try setting realistic goals. This can help.

TIME IS OF THE ESSENCE
What it means to be punctual.

Everyone seems to have their interpretation about being on time. Some consider on-time as arriving one-half hour early, and others, coming an hour after the expected arrival time, is also on time. According to Wikipedia, each culture seems to have its acceptable degree of punctuality.

More often, a small amount of lateness is acceptable, ten to fifteen minutes in Western cultures. Japanese society expects much stricter adherence to arrival times. Some cultures have an unspoken understanding that actual start times are different from stated start times. For example, people turn up for an event an hour later than invited. In this case, since everyone understands that a 9 pm party will start at around 10 pm, no one is inconvenienced when everyone arrives at 10 pm.

My experience has a more personal feeling. To me, being late is a sign of disrespect.

There are two points of view on this. It's power vs. vulnerability. The late person shows dominance over the other by making them wait, and the waiting person loses power by being made to wait. Let me illustrate this:

My mother (it's always my mother!) made an appointment to meet me on a Saturday morning after my dance lesson at the entrance to Lord & Taylor department store on Fifth Ave. I was about 12 years old.

I got there at the appointed time and started to scrutinize incoming customers, scanning faces to see hers. There was a clock on the wall, so I watched the minutes turn into hours — no mom. When I got tired of standing, I found a fire hydrant right in the lobby with a flat top and sat on it.

Still no, Mom.

I didn't dare leave for fear that she would arrive and not find me. After an hour or so, I had to pee but felt constrained from leaving to go to the Ladies Room. My impatience grew into despair.

I was a prisoner of Lord & Taylor's lobby without a jailor. None was needed because my jailor was me, imprisoned by my mother, who was someplace else. I know what I'll do, I thought. I'll leave and take the subway home. But, she would have become frantic by my absence, thinking some sex-craved maniac had captured me.

I was in Hell.

Finally, she arrived, over two hours late and without any explanation or apology. When I confronted her about her lateness, she sloughed it off by saying she had been busy. What she didn't say was that I wasn't important enough for her to worry about. She took for granted I would be there, awaiting her arrival, not caring about the anxiety she engendered in me.

When I was older and had just started dating, I agreed to meet this guy, another counselor I had met at camp, in the lobby of the old Astor hotel. He lived in New Jersey, and I lived in uptown Manhattan. It was our first date, and our parents knew each other.

I wore a new dress, wore stockings and high heels, wore make-up, and carried a purse. I waited over an hour, becoming more and more agitated. The hotel manager came over and asked me if I was waiting for someone. I felt embarrassed to be approached by him as if I was a loiterer. When I told him yes, he asked me to go to the balcony overlooking the lobby to be not mistaken for a prostitute looking for any date. A prostitute? Me? My red-face and I complied. I suffered through another thirty minutes and then took the subway home, trembling during the entire trip. I was seventeen at the time.

A beautiful bouquet with an apology note arrived two days later. That helped, but I refused to meet this guy again (even though he was cute.) The circumstances were different from my Lord & Taylor ordeal, but my feelings were the same. I was a prisoner with a built-in jailor who couldn't leave, couldn't pee, with massive anxiety as my partner.

On the other hand, I have a friend who is usually an hour late every time we have an appointment. There is no underlying message here. She can't get her act together. I don't take her lateness to be an indication of my worthlessness. I once told her that I was deducting one whole year from our relationship of fifty-five years for lateness. We both laughed about it.

Of course, since almost everyone has a mobile phone, the anxiety factor is eliminated these days. Either party can call the other to explain.

What a relief!

However, mobile phones don't remove the possible underlying motives of the late-comer. It could be disorganization, starting to get ready too late, not caring about the other person's time, or a display of superiority over a meet-up they plan to control. If you plan to be late, you can just as easily plan to be on time. Ask yourself if you tend to come to events late; Why are you doing this?

The answer may reveal how you rate yourself against other people and may encourage being more considerate.

WHAT WERE THE WORST DECISIONS OF YOUR LIFE?
These are some of the bad choices I have made.

Looking back, I can find three decisions that changed the course of my existence. At the time I made these decisions, they felt OK. But, through the "retrospecto-scope," I can see these refusals closed doors I would have benefited by walking through.

Here's the first one: It has to do with dance.

I started dancing when I was about three years old. I love to dance. Moving my body through the air fluidly, sometimes gracefully — sometimes not, sometimes with music — sometimes without, fills my soul with joy.

As a teenager, I studied dance with Hanya Holm. She was one of the founders of the US modern dance movement. Holm's technique enforced the importance of pulse, planes, floor patterns, aerial designs, and spatial dimensions. Her approach emphasized the freedom and flowing quality of the torso and back.

Her technique put words and structure to my innermost feelings about how to move. It was a combination of intellect and motion that appealed to me.

By now, you must be wondering, so, where's the mistake?

When I was in college, I lived in a sorority house that employed a student House Boy. He was a dancer, and when he learned of my knowledge of the Hanya Holm method, he said, "I'm starting a dance group. Why don't you come and join us?" His name was Paul Taylor, the famous Paul Taylor. His dance troupe was formed in1954 and performed all over the world. I refused the offer. How different would my life have been if I had said yes?

By that time, I had decided that the dance world would not fulfill my dreams. The phrase, "Up a steep and very narrow stairway," written by Edward Kleban, the lyricist for A Chorus Line, described part of the backstage world of dance.

But, atop the narrow staircases was the squalor of dressing rooms, the dirt and roaches skittering around. I didn't love that part of the equation. How shallow was that? There were other reasons I said no to this outstanding opportunity.

My family functioned better when I was at home, so I always had to return ASAP after completing my final exams. I was allowed out of the house for academic pursuits only. Once completed, I felt compelled to return to the dysfunctional household I had temporarily escaped at college.

I felt too restrained by my responsibilities at home to commit to demanding extracurricular activities.

And, added to those reasons, I was scared to death that I wasn't good enough.

My next mistake had to do with Bloomingdale's.

Even before I graduated, Bloomingdale's hired me for their Executive Training Squad. It was a great job that would lead me directly to an exciting long-term career. After completing that first part of my employment, I became the Assistant Buyer in the Hosiery department.

My boss was terrific and included me in all vendor activities, lunches, and outings at famous and expensive places. What fun!

During that period, Maggie de Mille was the Fashion Director of Bloomingdale's, who had a few young women assistants. I was getting ready to leave my job, but management tried to convince me to stay. They offered me a job as one of Maggie de Mille's assistants.

Can you believe I turned it down? It was a terrible decision. I would have flourished under de Mille's direction.

My at-the-time boyfriend said he would take me skiing if I didn't have to work on Saturdays. So I gave up this fantastic opportunity. And we never went skiing, besides. Instead, we broke up.

What a jerk I was.

My next mistake happened when I lived in Providence, R.I.

I was a member of B'nai Brith, a prominent Jewish women's charity organization. A local TV station invited us to attend its morning show, and the producer needed someone to read the weather report during the program. The regular weather girl was absent that day.

I think they selected me because I was wearing a gorgeous green dress. So, I read it. After the show was over, the producer invited me to discuss employment.

I refused the invitation.

At that time, I had three little children at home and a difficult, cranky husband. The opportunity to say yes tempted me, but I had prioritized my life's choices, and being a TV weather girl didn't fit the picture. So maybe this last one was not so much a mistake but rather a disappointment.

Mistakes generally don't lead to permanent self-destruction. The human spirit for survival, allows us to manipulate our lives to make sure we can develop an alternative plan.

We have the power to modify our original objective.

WHAT'S SCARIER THAN ANGER?
For me, expressing anger is a tricky business.

I stumbled upon a rerun of the TV program MOM the other night in which Allison Janney's character, Mom, exhibits anger toward her husband, Adam, played by William Fichtner.

I realized I would never in my life have the guts to do what she did.

She and her husband were fighting in their bedroom. She got so angry that she scooped up her pillow and a blanket and slammed out of the room. She slept the night on the sofa with their dog. I marveled that she acted on her anger in such a direct way.

Throughout my lifetime, anger was absent from my emotional repertoire.

My second husband complained about my never showing rage or anything even near annoyance with him. I guess you miss psychic pain if it's what you are accustomed to.

My first husband was such a tower of rage himself that I feared if I showed any displeasure over his behavior, his fury would have been downright dangerous. Trust me; any woman would have been enraged by his catalog of issues.

But I think my fear of being angry started from my earliest childhood, so I can't blame it on my first marriage. Where it began resides in a foggy memory.

Can such early memories be accurate? I wonder.

I seem to remember my father threatening to hit me with his belt because I wouldn't stop crying. I cried because I wanted to join a party in the other room instead of being in a dark room and told to go to sleep. He appeared as a dark silhouette taking up most of the doorway to my room lit from behind. He was un-buckling his belt as he stood there. I stopped crying from fear. I don't remember that he hit me, but it feels ominous, even today.

By the time I was four or five, pacifier's traits were a part of me. I lived in the same building as my cousin, and whenever she was mad at me (like always, it seemed), I was desperate to soothe her displeasure, to make it disappear.

During one of these angry fits, she stormed off to her bedroom, vanishing from my sight, leaving a space where she had been, and slammed the door behind her. I needed to see her, ensuring she hadn't vanished permanently. I started after her to fix everything when her mother, my aunt, said to me, "Why don't you let her come to you instead of going first all the time?"

Good question! Why didn't I?

I rarely feel anger. The impulse is buried way before it gets to the realized level. Expressing my anger feels like I'm placing myself in danger. So, why would I do that? It's safer to suck it up.

If I'm the recipient of someone else's anger, I might be hit, abandoned, or the victim of some other retaliatory punishment. Since I'm not the scriptwriter for anyone but myself, I have no control over what they might do next. I can't take that risk; it's too frightening. Bullies have nothing to worry about from me.

Here's what I could have done about my cousin's slamming the door on me. (Can you imagine — this idea just came to me, eighty-three years too late.) I could have gone home. Then, when she left her room and found me gone, she might have realized that her actions had consequences. She was the number one bully in my life for a long time. Now, we have zero contact with each other.

I'm an expert at controlling my own emotions, so no problem in that department. Or so I thought until I started having panic attacks.

My panic attacks felt like I had taut guitar strings attached to my esophagus, being plucked, vibrating in waves down the midline of my chest, accompanied by not breathing and being overtaken by fear. Therapy helped me to see that unexpressed anger was the basis of these episodes. And, I haven't been troubled with them recently.

My solution to dealing with this dark quirk of my personality is to bracket its power emotionally. Its time-out effect allows me to figure out who's mad at whom. It's an effective technique for dealing with any "downer" things. Bracketing allows me to be happy. It's like saying, "This is a bad situation, but I can deal with it some other time." Putting up these brackets is the Scarlet O'Hara Solution.

You may do the same sort of thing. If you do, welcome to this adaptive organizing system.

YOU CAN REINVENT YOURSELF: TAKE A DIFFERENT PATH
Here's a way to adapt for the sake of survival.

Reinventing oneself is a life's choice. It's another word for adapting/pivoting, the newest word. At any time, when faced with seemingly insurmountable daily problems, a person can decide to change course and try something new.

I know it's easier to say than to do, having done it myself several times.

According to Darwin's Origin of Species, it is not the most intellectual of the species that survives; it is not the strongest that survives, but the species that survives can best adapt and adjust to the changing environment it finds itself.

I've always lived with one foot in an artsy world and the other in a business one. As a girl, I loved to dance and studied with Hanya Holm, a German pioneer in Modern Dance. I also studied music privately and at Music and Art High School, where I played the french horn. After college, my first job was on the Executive Training Squad of Bloomingdale's, representing the "other foot." I couldn't seem to make a full commitment to one side or the other.

So, I got married! It was my first reinvention.

At least it was a full commitment and what I thought I was supposed to do. Hubby was always troubled; I knew that before I married him. My family home situation, however, was worse, and I needed an escape. And, for sure, hubby and I had some good times together. During these years, I had become a photographer, had a darkroom, studied at the International Center of Photography in NYC, and had started working as a school photographer. I raised three children. I thought of myself as a supermom.

As time went on in my marriage, my husband, being troubled, became impossible to live with and started taking his growing anger out on our children. After 20 years of being married to him, I sued him for divorce.

Getting unmarried was my next reinvention.

I became a divorcee. I was no longer bullied and managed to have lots of fun. I had to give up being a photographer due to a lack of funds. So, I went to an employment agency to look for a job and ended up working for that agency as a recruiter in the computer world, of which I knew nothing.

My next reinvention!

I stayed in that career for almost 15 years, but I never liked it. By the time the 1987 recession was in full swing, my business was not doing well, and I found a newspaper ad seeking people to be part/time phone reps at an international manufacturing company. I thought I could still handle my recruiting business and, at the same time, answer 800# calls. So I applied and was hired.

Another reinvention.

The next 12 years went by very quickly. I remarried, advanced myself to become a full/time worker at my job, and was promoted to Supervisor. But, as all things do, the position came to an end, and one of my children said, **"Mom, don't retire to do nothing. It's not good for you."**

You guessed it — another reinvention.

I decided to become a Life Coach and, at the same time, a Leader of group meetings at a prominent weight loss company by the end of the following year. I accomplished both. It was a challenging time, and I needed to do both. I loved doing these jobs, but the weight loss company laid me off due to COVID-19, and there were too few coaching clients forthcoming to be a significant part of my life no matter how hard I tried to find them.

And now what to do? Of course, I've become older and older and need to reinvent myself, my options are more limited than they used to be. So, I'm becoming a Blog writer, hopefully, successful.

This last is my newest reinvention — a Writer!

So the point of this story is to urge you to adapt and reinvent yourself when necessary. As you can see from the Darwin quote, adaptability is the path to survival. You have the power to create a new reality

SECTION TWO:
THE BENEFITS AND INCONVENIENCES OF AGING

Cut loose your consciousness from the body.
Use it no more to accept limitations.

– Parmahansa Yogananda

A JOB? FOR ME?
Is it possible there's a job out there I can still do?

I have an attitude about labor that works for me and always has. Working connects me to the world. I like getting a salary. When I'm working, I feel I am a functional part of society. The amount of my earnings almost doesn't matter — what matters is that another person or company values what I do enough to give me money to do it. Wow!

I had a few summer jobs during my college years, as my kids would ask, "That was that right after the Civil War, right?" Well, no!

I sold handkerchiefs in Orbach's Department store one summer and sold more than 500 in one day. It was a record-breaker. A handkerchief is a piece of cloth used to wipe your nose (for those of you who are too young and know of them.)

Another was a job with the Tommy Pajama Company. Computers were yet to arrive, so in my position, I totaled each customer's order mentally. Any mistake I made would affect their bill. I was an expert at adding quarter dozens and had challenged myself to how many more customer's orders I could complete in each hour. My bosses were tickled and asked me to come back as a full-time employee when I graduated.

I love being in a contest, even if no other person is competing. I declined the offer because I saw no future in it.

Instead of added numbers, my full-time job was with Bloomingdale's on their Executive Training Squad.

It was a great job. It felt like a continuation of my college years as my co-workers were new graduates, too. I ultimately became the Assistant Buyer of the Hosiery department.

Those summer jobs were the beginning. Now, I'm at the other end of my work curve, and I feel about the same about working as I did then. I had lots of different jobs in between then and now. I valued most of my jobs even though I never was a top earner.

It was a surprise when I learned about a job that I am perfectly qualified for last week. That is, qualified except for the fact that I'm going to be 89 years old in May. I'm also surprised that I applied for this job.

Some nerve, applying for a job at my age!

The potential employer doesn't know my exact age, and I'm not planning to spread that news. However, since I had to send a picture, they know I'm not young anymore. It will be an even bigger surprise if they want to interview me. The only problem I see with this potential adventure is whether I want to start working again, even though it's only a part/time job. The pandemic caused my lay-off almost a year ago. I don't want anything to interfere with my blog writing. I'm home all the time. I live in a high-rise, so my big daily event is going to the lobby for my mail. If offered, I could easily fit this job into my schedule. However, I would have to modify the amount of time I spend doing jigsaw puzzles and reading books. Also, what happens to my naps?

Rather than stressing, I'm going to chill. It's hard for me to do that since I'm a little obsessive. Waiting for something that might or might not happen is like watching out for the next snowstorm.

Should I wear my snow boots or my regular shoes?

ET STANDS FOR EXTRATERRESTRIAL AND WHAT ELSE?
Having an Essential Tremor (ET) is another life challenge.

Being physically challenged is to be expected as the years go on, and as we all realize, the other alternative is worse. So, this message is, "How do I approach these confrontations with adaptive skills that increase rather than diminish my existence"? It's not easy. It's an old cliche but still valid, "Old Age Is Not For Sissies."

According to the Mayo Clinic, an "Essential tremor is a nervous system (neurological) disorder that causes involuntary and rhythmic shaking. It can affect almost any part of your body, but the trembling occurs most often in your hands — especially when you do simple tasks, such as drinking from a glass or tying shoelaces".

The first time I noticed the problem was at the beginning of a required pen and pencil test (you know, writing essay answers to questions on a yellow legal pad) that I had to take to become a Certified Life Coach. I was so nervous that as I started to write, my hand involuntarily began to tremble fiercely. To make it stop, I had to clamp my left hand on top of my quaking right hand. That worked, my hand stopped convulsing, and I went on to complete this two-hour test without further incident. I chalked it up to anxiety. Yes, I passed! My trembling happened in 2005.

As the years went on, I would encounter a similar situation and not always related to my emotional state. I tried to assist with serving the soup course at a friend's Passover Seder meal. On my way to the table, my right hand and arm began their usual dance pattern, and the soup went flying. Everyone, except for the spilled-on guests, thought it was amusing. I was barred from serving soup.

Believe it or not, I began to find these incidents funny.

It is a bizarre event when no matter how hard one tries and fails to control the movement of one's hand, it has to be viewed with a sense of humor.

There seems to be no way to predict when these episodes will occur. After the event is over, I analyze its components to determine if there is any pattern to their onset. If I can find patterns, I can avoid them.

But, they remain bizarre.

So, OK, my hands shake. Not fatal — and sometimes goofy. And, yes, my left hand is also involved but way less than my right.

My ET has now become more obvious and annoying because my handwriting is affected. It is almost impossible for me to create a curvy line without it coming out wobbly. So, no more cursive writing; printing will have to do. It's a weird feeling to lose this skill after having it since kindergarten. Ironically, my penmanship grades (yes, we got grades for penmanship) in elementary school never were higher than mediocre. So you could say I couldn't write legibly even when I could write.

I know what I'll do. I'll create a new font that has no curvy lines.

Like my name, LYNN, it will be all straight lines and angles. That will make my life much less demanding. Even though my straight lines might turn out with little wiggles in them, and my slants might erupt into wild unruly lines, this attempt at control is my way to adapt.

I had to write a message on a greeting card recently but didn't want to embarrass myself by writing it out. So I typed it on my computer, selected a pretty typeface, and a fetching color for the printing. Then I printed what I had written, cut the paper to fit the card's size, and taped it on. It looked way better than if I had handwritten it. This is another adaptive technique.

My only problem now is writing my signature. Maybe I'll have a stamp created so that I can sign checks.

The bottom line then is to use my imagination and humor to find ways to solve age-related inconveniences. Taking care of the obligations demanded by a chronic illness also can be satisfied this same way.

HEAR, HEAR! WHAT'S THAT YOU SAID?
The significance of hearing losses in one's life is monumental.

Most of us are born with all our senses intact. It's a blessing. And most of us experience a lessening of these excellent faculties as we age and, that's a bummer.

The proof of the pudding.

I was one of the fortunate who had, from birth, wonderfully sharp hearing, seeing, tasting, touching, and smell. The Music and Art High School test consisted of proficiency in either music or art but also had a physical element. During the try-out, one of the tasks was to listen to three tones through a head-set and determine whether the middle sound was the same, higher, or lower than the others. These tones ranged from upper registers to lower ones and were close in sound to each other. It wasn't easy.

After I completed the test, I accompanied the student monitor who carried my results to the admission office, and the monitor told me I had a perfect score. Of course, I couldn't take any credit for that since that was how I was born — with excellent hearing.

On the proficiency side, I auditioned by playing Beethoven's Country Dances on the piano. I played the first two pages well, but when I got to the top of the third page, my hands froze for unknown reasons, and I couldn't play another note. I just sat there, trembling. The auditioner was a kind person and allowed me to try it again.

(I was accepted, hurrah, and spent the next four years playing the French Horn. We all had to play a second instrument. Music and Art High School was one of the specialized high schools in New York City. It was fabulous.)

So, time passed, and, gradually, so did my hearing.

Years later, during my working years in my sixties, I thought my hearing was adequate. I noticed, however, that I frequently had to ask people to repeat themselves. I could mostly hear and understand everyone, except when the conversation turned to gossip, fascinating gossip. At that point, the volume of the conversation lowered, as did my comprehension. It was so frustrating. Missing out on the latest juicy news wasn't any fun at all.

At the same time, I found that I wasn't able to have conversations with my grandchildren because I couldn't understand one word of what they said. It saddened me and prompted me to seek help from an audiologist, and, sure enough, I needed hearing aids.

Here's my pet peeve.

Hearing aids are expensive, and Medicare has made the decision not to pay for them. It has also made a decision not to pay for eyeglasses. How frustrating is that? If Medicare is supposed to cover the medical needs of the over 65 set, aren't these devices near the top of the needs list? Many people can't afford them. I know they are not medical but consider this scenario. A visually impaired person or one who may not hear well may be hit by a vehicle while attempting to cross the street. Medicare then might have expensive bills to pay for the victim's recovery. Wouldn't it be more prudent to prevent the incident in the first place? Their decision doesn't make sense.

WHO estimates that unaddressed hearing loss costs the global economy US$ 750 billion annually due to health sector costs (excluding the cost of hearing devices), prices of educational support, loss of productivity, and societal costs.

My hearing is now seriously impaired.

I've been wearing hearing aids for sixteen years. I'd be lost without them. I reach for them as soon as I get out of bed and wear them all day long. They are a link to my connection with the rest of the world. In group activities, there are times when the conversation is too fast and too soft for me to comprehend the content.

My choice is to ask my friends and family to speak louder and slower, and they are more than willing to do so. After the next few minutes, the conversation returns naturally to its former volume and speed, and I am lost. I can't ask them again because I know the same thing will happen.

So, I remain seated, smile, and nod when everyone else does, without knowing what I'm smiling and nodding about. I have to act like I can understand the conversation when I can't follow it at all. Not hearing well separates one from the flow of dialogue. Isolation, and sometimes boredom, is the result. After a while, loneliness sets in, and brain function diminishes.

Hearing loss is associated with Alzheimer's disease and dementia. The risk increases with the hearing loss degree. Several hypotheses, including cognitive resources being dependent on hearing and social isolation resulting from hearing loss, are potential outcomes. According to Thomson RS, Auduong P, Miller AT, Gurgel RK (April 2017). "Hearing loss as a risk factor for dementia: A systematic review."

The use of hearing aids can diminish the severity of dementia. According to preliminary data, in an article by Hoppe U, Hesse G (2017–12–18). "Hearing aids: indications, technology, adaptation, and quality control hearing aid usage can slow down the decline in cognitive functions."

Masks are a challenge.

I generally understand one on one conversations because I have learned to lip-read. Since COVID and masks, though, I'm just out of luck. I've lost about 50% of my comprehension by not being able to watch someone's mouth as they speak. Also, since my hearing aids rest behind my ears, my mask's elastic bands push my hearing aids aside. Then, frequently added to that are the sides of my sunglasses, also behind my ears. Can you imagine that each of the items, hearing aids, elastic bands, and sunglasses, are fighting with each other for supremacy in that tiny space? Well, that's what I'm sensing. It's ridiculous!

I hope that once we are all vaccinated, we won't need masks. But, who knows when that will be, if ever.

You can see that I've gone from the top of the hearing heap down to my current level. There are people with worse hearing than I'm currently experiencing. I understand that, and I feel sorry for them. I'm doing the best I can and try to have realistic expectations. Life is challenging, and happily, I'm still able to put up a good fight.

HOW MANY POSITIVES CAN YOU FIND ABOUT OLD AGE?
Believe it or not, there are many.

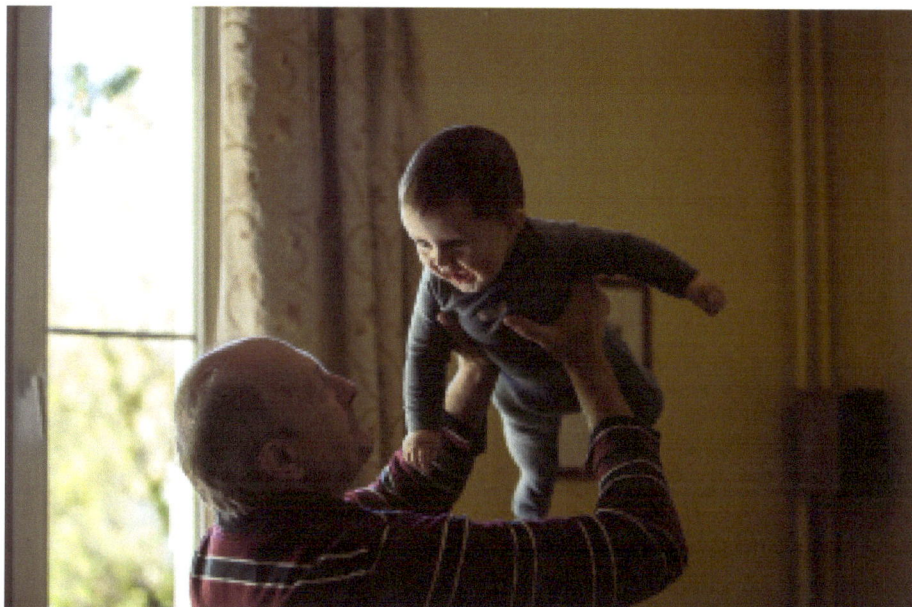

What does being old mean to you? Is it your actual age or your connection to the world? Or is it your health, what you see in the mirror, or something else entirely?

When I've tried to answer this question, I realized that being old has many more good aspects than I thought. Surprisingly I've found more positives than negatives.,

WISDOM is my number one! I'm a lot smarter than I used to be. The knowledge I've accumulated over the years seems to have rearranged itself in my brain into broad categories with subtitles and sub-sub titles. In other words, applying what I have learned throughout my life is now available for me to use in situations that arise today.

Socrates, however, wouldn't have agreed with that since he said, "The only true wisdom is in knowing you know nothing." I guess he would say humility counts. You may wish to read an informative article entitled "Does Wisdom Come With Age?" by Stephen L. Antczak, April 30, 2018, on "nextavenue" for a review of writings on the subject of wisdom.

Next on my list of positives is the accomplishment of STILL BEING ALIVE. You know, regardless of everything else, if you're reading this — good for you! Then there is GRATITUDE. I'm thankful for my energy. There are many other things I'm grateful for, the people in my life, my physical surroundings, but too many to list.

Next on my list are the GENES I inherited. They are working out pretty well. Then, there is the opportunity of TRYING NEW THINGS. There is nothing that can put me in the same space every day other than myself. I hold the key to my life. Writing these blogs is so much fun and new for me.

Being around for so long allows me to SATISFY MY CURIOSITY. What I mean by that is I like to find out how things are going, such as with my children, with elections, how successful (or not) we are with Covid-19, and with recipes I haven't tried yet.

And finally, I have a greater SENSE OF FREEDOM than I ever had in my life. I'm way less bound to what other people might think of what I have to say. I can go to bed anytime I wish; I can get out of bed when my eyes open, not forced by an alarm clock. I can do with my life anything that my health will allow.

So this last is a perfect segue to the negatives of being old.

I find that most people are NOT INTERESTED IN WHAT I HAVE TO SAY. I tell stories from my past that I feel illustrate some point I am trying to make about a current event. Some folks are tolerant because they love me, but most just interrupt me. I am not interested in forcing my stories, so I just close my mouth and make-believe everything is fine.

I'm not INVISIBLE. Sometimes when I'm sitting with a group of mixed age people, the conversation is active. I wish to participate. So I start speaking, and everyone in the room stops and listens to me. No one takes issue with my statement or responds in any way. They just start talking again precisely at the point where they were as if I had not said anything at all. It's another make-believe everything is a "fine" moment.

Then the HEALTH circumstances we find ourselves in are significant. I deal with a bunch, some related to age and some not. The age-related ones are annoying. My hearing is not good. I use hearing aids, but they don't replicate normal hearing. My heart valves are leaking, and my bladder, and worst of all, I have shortness of breath. Oh no, the worst one is the lessening of my former strength. Good thing I have a doorman to open jars and bottles of Scotch.

Lastly, the MIRROR — it's consistently shocking. The latest issue for me, since I'm wearing a mask when I leave my house, is whether or not to put on make-up. I look better with make-up (that truly means younger), but so much of my face is hidden; it doesn't seem worth the effort. Then again, my eyes show so I can use eye make-up, and I must constantly draw on my missing eyebrows!

So the score is seven positive to four negative. There are almost double the good to the bad.

I'd say that being old has more advantages than we may have thought.

Why not think up your list and analyze your life. Your analysis may bring you to a better way of spending every day for the rest of your life.

IS THIS THE COMPLAINT BUREAU?
Am I being cheated out of my life in retirement?

I have always enjoyed being immersed in the good life and wasn't particularly looking for a life of leisure. By leisure, I mean loafing around, doing jigsaw puzzles, reading mystery novels, re-organizing my underwear drawer, and my all-time favorite, taking naps. Once in a while, doing a YouTube exercise tape also qualifies.

Leisure is my life now.

My before-leisure life was focused on part/time work (for which I got paid) and participating in other activities. I took flute, acting lessons and participated in a Play Reading group that satisfied my artsiness. I volunteered at The Jewish Home twice a week in a program for residents who have dementia. That fulfilled my commitment as a giving person. I went to the gym in my co-op about 4-5 times a week and had a four-concert subscription to the NJ Symphony with friends, including pre-concert dinners in restaurants. I was busy.

I am old, but I believe that stimulating activities are vital to maintaining youth and vigor. Hugging people is also.

So, that's why I'm looking for the complaint department. It's one thing to be halfway through your life and be semi-quarantined, but quite another when your life is coming to an end sooner. When you're in one of the middle-age categories, there are probably many more years ahead of you, so giving up a year of activities may not be as crucial for you. I know, being able to participate in life's choices is crucial at any age, but it's a more significant deficit when you're an old/oldster. Who listens to folks like me?

You can aspire to a younger age level if your attitude includes courage, openness to challenges, and not finding glory or excuses in saying or even thinking,

"I'm too old to do that." Since my 89th birthday is coming up in May, you can figure out where I am.

Here's how I've divided up the years:
        20–27, young/Young
        28–35, medium-aged/Young
        36–40, old/Young
        41–53 young/Middle-aged
        54–62 middle/Middle-aged
        63–70 old/Middle-aged
        71–78 young/Oldster
        79–87 middle-age/Oldster
        88–105 old/Oldster
        106–who knows/Ancient

So, you see, old/Oldsters may not have too many years left. Giving up a year (so far) of my precious remaining years is cruel. I've lost the uncut version of my 2020 existence.

Maybe I'm missing my last chance to see Barcelona!

I am not minimizing how younger people are affected. Everyone is suffering but in different ways. It just feels that because of my age, I need to expand, not diminish my space, to put my arms around everything and everyone I love now. Tomorrow may be too late.

That's why I'm looking for the complaint bureau. I'm sick of staying home alone.

IT'S PROBLEMATIC NOT KNOWING WHEN YOU'LL DIE
Here's a look at an often-ignored subject.

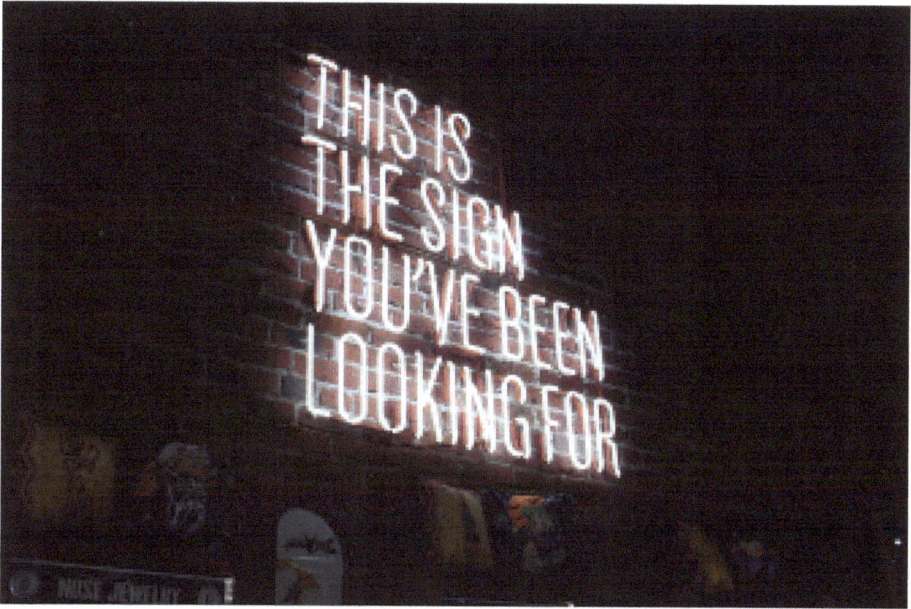

First of all, we must eliminate from our discussion those who are suffering from fatal diseases. We are sorry you are ill and pray for a speedy resolution of your pain. Rather, I'm speaking to a separate audience, those of us who are old and go along from day to day, not particularly in top-shelf condition, but getting along Okay.

Stress over when we'll die begins to appear in our 70s and grows as the years go on.

For me, nearing 89 years old, the concept of dying has become a part of my imagination, not so much how it will happen, but when it will happen. Much has been written on near-death signs. Not so much on the biggest secret of secrets, the time and place of our actual demise.

I began to imagine a totally different world.

In this new world, everyone would be born, carrying in their bodies the total amount of nourishment needed for their lifetimes. It would be something like an internal backpack that automatically diminishes as we grow and age. Everyone would understand when our internal food supply was exhausted and our lives would end. From time to time, a government food agency would measure us, and we would get an accurate reading of the amount of time left to us — no anxiety, just facts.

It would be so helpful to know when it will happen. We would know when to stop buying new clothing — when to start eating forbidden foods — when to go on a trip to a place we've longed to visit (probably sooner rather than later), and whether or not we should buy formal wear for our grandchildren's weddings.

Everything would be so much clearer about our future if we knew our Death-day (opposite of Birthday.). If we knew the date of our ending, we could plan

Deathday parties and participate in them and celebrate our lives.

The downside of this plan would be eliminating food as we know it, not necessarily beverages. We would continue to imbibe beverages like water and scotch. I would miss the food, having creamy cheeses, crunchy nuts, sturdy steaks, and just about everything I put in my mouth to eat.

No such things as pizza or Chinese Food would exist.

This plan would eliminate the food chain, our greatest gift from the universe, since we are at the top of it.

The plan, while fun to contemplate, has too many negatives.

Not knowing when we'll die leaves us with uncertainty and tension. We all know of instances of sudden, unexpected deaths. My grandfather died at his son's wedding after having danced all night. Another man I knew dropped dead while dancing at a Christmas party.

(I never thought of dancing as life-threatening, but there you go!)

Given a choice, don't you think they would have selected different times? Granted, these deaths were the best for them but left their families in shock and disbelief.

What about all our stuff — not just clothing but real estate, bank accounts, valuable articles, government obligations, and junk to discard? I think it's unfair to our heirs to vanish from their lives, leaving them with a frustrating treasure hunt — no clues about how to find anything. Decisions need to be made.

So, how do we eliminate some of this anxiety about when we die? I believe planning and organizing will be a step forward.

First, select a person(s) you can trust and who is willing to take on this role.

1. *Create a will, a living will, a power of attorney document, and a health proxy; (you've probably done this already.)*
2. *Make lists of every asset (where they are kept and how to access them), including Social Security, income sources, interest, stockbrokers, etc.*
3. *Add every liability (what you owe and to whom), monthly maintenance, mortgage payment, whatever.*
4. *List credit cards (with account numbers, user names, and passwords).*
5. *Write which bills are paid automatically and which are paid regularly by check or online.*
6. *Add whatever insurance you have, auto, homeowners, and health. Be specific with policy numbers, types, and carriers, including contact information. Include your Medicare number and secondary insurance, and long-term care policy.*
7. *Add your doctors (include specialties), phone numbers, addresses.*
8. *Include your SSN# and where it's kept.*

Congratulate yourself when you've finished. Perfect is not the goal. Remember having something written down is better than nothing,

Keep a copy of your list for yourself and send a copy to the person(s) you've previously chosen. Keep it accurate. Make changes when they occur. You can do this online or with paper and pencil. It's a lot of work but worth the effort. My list is several years old and is as accurate as I can make it. It's a comfort.

Second, do a systematic cleanout, closet by closet.

Eliminate any articles that really belong in the garbage. Do your kids a favor. I keep at this, but I'm not as up-to-date as I would like. But I keep tossing stuff out.

Third — that's it! I haven't a clue what more I can do.

Except for reminding us all that every day is precious and doesn't come around twice. So even with our pandemic rules for living, make sure you take care of yourself both physically and emotionally every day.

Don't just try to have fun (trying is a way of not doing), rather plan and execute a fun thing to do for each day.

MY LIFE; BATTERIES REQUIRED
How various batteries and other devices keep me going.

I have devices that let me know when something in my body is about to fall apart. Gone are the carefree days when my body worked by itself, without even thinking about it. And I say thank you to the brilliant minds that created all my stuff. And, thank you to all the manufacturers who do the producing. And while I'm at it, thank you to the shipping companies that bring most of these items to my local stores.

As a Type 1 Diabetic, I use an insulin pump.

The pump is a small computer that sets aside space for an insulin reservoir within it. I wear this contraption 24/7 so that it can infuse me with medication. It is extremely accurate and can supply tiny amounts, which would be impossible to measure in a syringe. Special tubing and insertion equipment that is poked into my abdomen allows insulin delivery. About every three days, I have to refill the reservoir and install new tubing. I used to give myself 3 to 4 insulin injections each day. This system allows me to stick myself only 1 time every 3 days.

Amazingly, the whole gadget is activated by one AA battery.

I was a slave to testing my blood glucose (BG) level about 8 to 9 times a day. That meant I had to stick my finger and draw blood each time. The drawn blood was placed on a test strip that fitted into another monitor, of course, battery-operated. It did the job, but eventually, every fingertip of both hands was black and blue. And it was excruciating.

Now I use a CGM (continuous glucose monitor), also battery-operated, which measures my BG every five minutes automatically. I can read these numbers anytime by waving a reader across a disc inserted into my arm. I replace this disc once every 2 weeks. Way better, right?

I'm done with making multiple holes in my body to obtain my BG numbers. My only responsibility is to order and reorder the discs so that I have them on hand and use the appropriate wire to plug the reader into the wall. Of course, my overriding responsibility is to control my BG, a 24/7 basis.

This is a new world for me. The use of this device has released me from the obligation of continually hurting myself to not hurting myself at all; no more black and blue fingertips. I'm so grateful that batteries exist to help me stay healthy.

This world is totally amazing!

My hearing is shot. So I wear hearing aids, battery-driven, every day from the time I wake up until I jump into bed. They are my links to the world. Without them, I would be totally isolated from my family and friends and, I fear, would be on the road to dementia.

It's totally frustrating to hear what people are saying without being able to comprehend any of it. It also is very boring when one is disengaged. Hearing aids are expensive and fragile. Special batteries power each one; these batteries expire about every three days. Annoyingly the batteries die on different days, so I am constantly changing one or the other. Also, I have to be sure I have plenty of batteries on hand and usually carry some with me wherever I go.

Luckily, when I had cataract surgery, it was a done deal. No batteries required! When I had knee replacement surgery, no batteries were required here either. Whew! But, my usual existence is battery-laden. There are two in each of my TV remote controls (I have three TVs), four in each of my flashlights (I have three flashlights,) a rechargeable battery in my dental Waterpik, a toothbrush, which is a plugin. Of course, my computer has the potential to be battery-operated as long as the battery is charged. My phone needs to be plugged in, as does my watch.

No matter how hard I try to keep everything running, I'm always out of power on some device.

Yesterday, when I left my apartment to go shopping, I forgot to take my watch off the charger. When I got home and checked the number of steps I walked, it was only 5%. Very disappointing when I knew I had walked my feet off traipsing through two supermarkets.

So what's to be done about all these batteries. Absolutely nothing. Today's world is blessed with plug-in power, portable power, and plenty of batteries to do the jobs we need to get done. Give your batteries a hug (just kidding). They are continuously improving our existence, and they are about the only thing you can't bug these days. And, the price of them is minuscule when compared with the functionality they provide.

SENIORS VS. TECHNOLOGY
Asking for computer help or any help makes me cringe.

Modern life often requires computers, and for senior citizens, this can be like a punishment. I've actually been using computers for years, but instead of getting easier, it gets more complicated by the day. Here's my latest exasperation:

I received an email from The Department of Labor in my state that requires me to respond by uploading about 15 pages of data onto the form they sent me. I know how to send a photo to someone. But attaching it to another form is another thing entirely.

Originally I thought this request was a scam, so before sending out my personal financial reports, I made a few calls to verify its authenticity.

I called my accountant, who hasn't yet called me back, my state representative's office, a friend who said she would ask her boyfriend because he knows everything, my children, who also know everything, and The Department of Labor. Mostly everyone thought it was a scam except for The Department of Labor. It took about 3 hours to make all these calls. It took them 36 hours to call me back.

The Supervisor at the labor department said it was not a scam and I should definitely comply with the request. Therefore, I removed the copy I made from the garbage pail and started working on it.

The first thing I did was to take an iPhone picture of each page I needed to attach. Then I had to review the pages to ensure they were legible and didn't cut off the page edges.

This was the first problem.

I got mixed up matching the photographs to the actual pages. Inadvertently, I had taken duplicate photos of some pages and not photographed others. And, my iPhone seemed to have rearranged their order (undoubtedly my fault.)

Another problem is that I have shaky hands, so I have to hold the phone against my midriff for stability. The pictures came out with the image looking wider at the bottom than at the top. They were weird-looking.

So far, I had spent another 1:15 minutes resulting in zero progress. I could have spent this amount of time doing something more fun — like eating, napping, or reading!

Then I decided to try to upload just one page as a trial. So, I moved one picture to my desktop. So far, so good. Then I opened the page of the document where it was supposed to upload. With great anticipation of success, I grabbed the picture from my desktop with my mouse and slid it over.

The result? The photo slid itself right back to where it started.

GRRRRR!

I didn't know what I was doing. So, I went to Google and asked for help. Once I figured out the best wording for the "How to" sentence, I got a basket full of answers, mostly unintelligible to me. My frustration rose along with my blood pressure.

At this point, I had spent another 2 1/2 hours dealing with this and was no closer to a solution than when I started.

Total hours so far: about 6 hours, plus the 36 hours waiting for the Department of Labor to call me back. This waiting time was not tranquil; anxiety and frustration filled every minute.

The gambit was up. I had to request support from one of my children. In this instance, my daughter.

She was charming in her response and offered to do the whole job for me. You can guess I said OK in a nanosecond.

Throughout my life, I have handled my affairs successfully on my own. My mother taught me that I had to rely on myself because no one else would save me. So I learned to be self-reliant and also learned to cling to this quality. That's why I am pained by the need to seek assistance. It nullifies my hard-won self-confidence.

My generation's folks had no exposure to today's rampant technology, and we are now awash in incredible automation. In the 1940s, schools were dealing with such things as the quality of our penmanship. In graduate school, my granddaughter, in the third grade, was learning about Venn diagrams at the same time as I was. I thought it was funny, but that's a sample of how much education has advanced.

Most of the time, I enjoy using my computer. But, every other day, something comes up that has me stumped.

What's a girl to do?

THE FIVE BEST THINGS ABOUT ME AND THE FIVE WORST
Here's the result of my self-evaluation journey.

This was harder to do than I thought it would be. I found it was easier to identify the best things and harder to dig out the worst. I'm trying to determine why.

Here are the best.

1. Reinventing myself is a quality I'm proud of. It's my disciplined upbringing that allows me to turn in a new direction. Thank you, mom! The most recent model of me is a writer headed in the direction of a memoir. By Sunday, I will have completed forty-four articles, one written every week from my job lay-off throughout the pandemic. I hope to create a legacy as a book to give away to friends and family. During its creation, I noticed my twists and turns. I've been a department store executive, show-room designer, photographer, consumer services supervisor, life coach, flutist,

pianist, dancer, recruiter. It's been 88+ yrs of living, so no wonder there are so many different me's.

2. I'm a loyal friend. My friends have been my champions way back from high school days. My three college roommates are still around, and we communicate regularly. I'm the fourth. I tell them I love them often. We reminisce without getting into the "good old days" which I don't favor. I believe in today. Other friends I've acquired over the years are so great. I'd be lonely without them all.

3. My curiosity has no limits. I follow my questions into research and from research into actions. I might take a course (zoom, of course, these days) or spend hours on my computer looking up solutions to my current mysteries. I like to find out what's happening, the latest information, and what's the potential for the future. How will it all turn out? Curiosity keeps me up-to-date. I'm even curious about how scary new experiences will feel, like facing surgery or moving to a new home.

4. Taking responsibility for my own happiness is a quality I didn't grow up with. I became aware of it in therapy when dealing with my husband's unhappiness and trying to "fix" his problems. I learned that not only was I not responsible for his state of being, but I was also totally in charge of my own. What a relief!! I started to have much more fun.

5. For an 88-year-old, I don't look too bad. My skin is wrinkled, but I'm relatively agile, can still follow a conversation (if it's loud enough), and I have good reasoning skills. For the last 20 years or longer, people told me they wanted to be me when they grew up. I used to think, "Oh no! Am I that old"? Now I realize it was a compliment, and I accept it as one, wrinkles included.

Okay, now for the harder part. The worst of me.

1. Passivity takes over. All it takes are a few angry words from a person I value to return me to my former totally passive state. I say OK to practically anything as long as yelling is attached to the command. I'm easily intimidated and fold like an accordion when that happens. It's a habitual response that I notice only after it's over. In other words, it's an automatic kick-back.

2. I'm very competitive and like to be at the top of the heap when I'm in a crowd. I think I overestimate myself; my ego is overblown.

3. Being liked is of paramount importance to me. Here's how that works in my ancient self. If I'm not liked, people will not want to be with me and eventually abandon me forever. This feeling doesn't float on the top of my consciousness. I dug it out of the garbage pail of my childhood operating systems, but its shadow is still with me.

4. I am not kind to my delusional brother during our weekly phone conversations. He has no one else in the world that befriends him, and he has destroyed any relationships he had with other family members. I'm it. Usually, the call lasts about one-half hour, during which he talks, and I say, "Uh-huh." On occasion, he says something so outrageous that I take issue with him. He talks over me immediately, and then I yell at him. I know he

is mentally ill, but he pushes me to the end of my rope too quickly. I'm left feeling very guilty.

5. I'm a show-off. I was never thought of as being smart when I was a child. However, as the years have proceeded, I seemed to be getting smarter and smarter. Maybe it comes from the accumulation of experiences I've attained as life goes on. At any rate, I show off my current analytic skills all the time, and it must not be pleasing to others. However, it feels super terrific to me.

So, that's it, the best and the worst. This analysis is challenging and very revealing. Why not give it a try? Make a list of your best and your worst qualities. You may be surprised about what pops up.

WHAT AM I DOING NEXT?
Suddenly, I'm unemployed.

It actually wasn't such a shock to me. My career with my former employer was a rocky road, although it did last for 16 years. My job entailed dealing with the public and while I tried, I didn't fit the corporate mold. I couldn't look 30 years younger — I could do 15 maybe — but not 30, and I was not to be muzzled into a corporate automaton. I really feel that my employer had been trying to get rid of me for a long time and COVID-19 gave it a legitimate way to lower the ax. There were about 120 others laid off at the same time.

I have worked without a break since 1980. For a year of my work, I was a school photographer. That was lots of fun. Then I became a recruiter, ultimately in my own business in the field called at that time, "data processing", — not so much fun. After that, I worked for a 12-year stint at a major worldwide manufacturing corporation. If I had started working with that company when I was younger than 60, I think I could have had a fine career. There, I was expected to use my own analytical skills to solve problems. My performance was valued.

But my career was so all over the place and started so late in my life, it never amounted to much. Before my working life, I did the regular stuff, including having three excellent children, 2 husbands, grandchildren, and great-grandchildren, and made lots of wonderful friends.

In my spare time, I learned to play the flute, not too well but I liked being actively involved with music. I've taken acting lessons; I really loved them. I was a black and white photographer with my own darkroom, went to lots of Broadway shows, concerts, and attended and gave lots of dinner parties. Simultaneously, along the way, I became a life coach which I tried very hard to make into a successful career, but it didn't happen. I volunteered at a nursing home and worked with dementia patients for several years and will continue. As soon as it is safe again, I plan to continue with these activities.

However, I can't complain. My life has been productive and really busy. And now, I'm still blessed with the energy to do something. But what? Has my life, so far, been sort of a rehearsal for my need to reinvent myself, yet again?

These are some of my personal barriers: my hands shake so my writing is pretty much illegible, I became a Type1 diabetic at around 60, requiring a 24/7 monitoring job. My artificial parts are one knee, two new lenses in my eyes, and inserting hearing aids. Society's expectations for me to act like an old person are also prevalent. Of course, I am old – 88 is old!

Maybe it's a slow realization that my next job will never happen.

I am really retired which points to the closing down of my life. Having a job, no matter how small, underscores one's usefulness to society. To me, a job is a personal validation of being part of the world, instead of a bystander. It gives structure to life. The money one earns no matter how little, supplies an objective nod to vitality. In other words, retirement is a bummer, from my point of view.

I found lots of methods for achieving happiness, online. The following online site has been helpful to me and maybe to will be to you as well: https://www.lifehack.org/articles/communication/live-beautiful-life-10-easy-steps.html

WHAT'S HAPPENING TO MY BODY?

Have you ever asked yourself how your body has shaped your life?

Here are some things to consider: your size, your sex, your age, your strength, your flexibility, and your health, and how much significance you give to other peoples' opinions of your physical being. Can others cause you to lose faith in yourself? Maybe the main question is: Does your image strengthen or diminish the "real" you. Does it help or hinder fulfilling your dreams?

Are you satisfied with the body you currently inhabit?

Until I became a pre-teen, the awareness of my body was limited. My friends and I played, and not one of us noticed our bodies. If I was hungry, I ate practically anything.

Olives and Chinese food were my favorites, with nuts and cheese coming as a close second. And eating lobsters were on the list sometimes, if offered. Another favorite was peppery noodles and cheese, my everyday comfort food.

As a kid, I went with my father to the original Chelsea market to buy uncommon cheeses. I remember those outings as being first-rate and exotic, cheeses from all over the world with tastings always available. Some were salty, and others piquant. They almost all tasted wonderful. I eagerly strode with my dad from one stall to the next and was fascinated by the assortment. Time flew by. Although we were Kosher at home, he deemed any cheese admissible, even though it didn't conform to the rules of Kashrut (what's kosher and what isn't.)

My body was the available vehicle to satisfy every need my brain could think of. That's what mattered. I walked and talked, and I took for granted all my senses even though I now understand they were outstanding. Naturally, puberty followed, and so, suddenly, I was introduced to my new body not by secretly studying my image but by comments from other people.

My body shape had significance in my decision not to study dance seriously. Ballet and modern dance require the ability to jump off the ground and stay airborne with lightness, called Ballon. Compared to my dance classmates, I looked too top-heavy to achieve it. I was not a skinny flat chested girl who danced as if to defy gravity.

In elementary school, we were preparing for an event that included my dancing. We were on a stage whose floor stood about four feet higher than the floor of the auditorium.

The Russian dance I was rehearsing required jumping from one foot to the other while crossing my arms in front of my body at shoulder height. My fledgling breasts were jiggling as I danced.

I paid no attention to my body until I noticed a few boys standing on the auditorium floor at the edge of the stage, staring up and under my crossed arms, leering at my breasts, poking each other with their elbows, and giggling.

I almost died from embarrassment.

I told my mother what happened, and we went out that night to buy a "training bra." For the rest of elementary school and all of high school, I wore a bra, on top of that an undershirt — then a blouse — and then a sweater or vest to completely camouflage the front of my body. My posture became stooped over, another hiding technique.

Then, mom told me I was getting too fat and to eat fewer potatoes, bread, and noodles. Which part of my body was still OK? The problem was I had too much flesh all over me. The word "flesh" took on repulsive overtones.

My body which had been reliable for meeting any challenge and fulfilling all my desires, had morphed into an encumbrance.

My confidence waned, being replaced by revulsion about how I looked.

It took over fifty years for me to recover from that teenage angst. Maybe similar experiences explain people's current interest in piercing and tattooing. Studies have shown that 62% of people who have had piercings have done so to express their individuality or the opposite, to connect with a group identity. To what lengths will you go to please other people?

Even though the old Testament (Leviticus 19:28) prohibits piercing or other body modifications because the body is god's creation, tattooing and body piercing are everywhere. Today, people choose to be tattooed for artistic, cosmetic, sexual, and sentimental reasons or beautify the image that looks to them too uninteresting to be loveable.

So, you are not necessarily stuck with your body. You can always change its shape, thinner or fatter, or decorate it in historical ways. Tattooing and body piercing have been around since the beginning of recorded history. However, if you choose one of these paths, be sure it's because you want the change, not because someone else is displeased with your appearance and has destroyed your confidence in yourself.

If your confidence needs rebuilding, here are a few ways to do it:

Tips for building self-confidence

1. Look at what you've already achieved. You may have lost confidence if you believe you haven't achieved anything.
2. Think of things you're good at. All of us have strengths and talents.
3. Set some goals. Make sure the goals are achievable and realistic.
4. Engage your brain in something other than yourself, like volunteer work. The rewards are greater than you can imagine.

During my Life Coach training, we were introduced to a set of Coaching principles. Here's the one that is relevant to this discussion:

Pain is unavoidable; suffering is optional.

In other words, we have the option of accepting that life, at times, brings us genuine pain: physical or emotional. The optional part might be adding internal self-talk, with thoughts like, "It's not fair, or why does this always happen to me? Or, if we are dealing with our body's aging and lessening of our faculties, it's better to accept the changes than being frustrated and vent our anger onto other people. You know, old and cranky!

Understanding the gallantry exhibited by older people who adapt to changes in their bodies deserves applause. And, teenage apprehensions about their bodies deserve no less. So, be kind to the young just getting started and the elderly at the opposite end of living. Congratulate them when you notice their equanimity.

SECTION THREE:
TIPS ON HOW TO LIVE BETTER

Tell me and I forget.
Teach me and I remember.
Involve me and I learn.

– Benjamin Franklin

THREE REASONS WHY COMPREHENDING EACH OTHER IS SO THORNY

Some tips on how to improve communication with those we love, and those that annoy us.

Growing up takes us from innocence to knowledge, from ignorance to responsibility, and from the process of adding more and more participation with life. Finally, we gain what we think of as being a grown-up. Our sense of reality gives us the confidence we need to succeed in life. What we believe to be true is valid to each of us. We accept. Everything we have learned arises from our ACCUMULATION OF ENCOUNTERS.

So, what's wrong with that?

Really nothing! As long as we live alone and never have a conversation with anyone. We KNOW what we KNOW. The only reality check for our thinking is us.

Problem #1:

Once we are conversing with someone else, we notice their ACCUMULATION OF ENCOUNTERS doesn't ever match ours. We are all unique. We are the total of our experiences, as they are a total of theirs. Our collection of biases and prejudices may clash with the other's stockpile of biases and prejudices in a conversation. How can we communicate with the "real" person lurking inside?

This idea was advanced by the noted Scottish psychiatrist, R.D. Laing, in the 1960s and 1970s. He said," I cannot experience your experience. You cannot experience my experience. We are both invisible men."

Sometimes, I wonder if there are no such things as the invisible man or woman. What if we are fluid entities that keep evolving as we continue to encounter new experiences.

The contents of the "real you" may be a moving target.

It's peculiar, but I can't tell if this is a good or bad thing. It's fun to explore the idea, either way. Think of some of the people you have known for many years. Are they the same as when you met them, or have they changed? Do you think there is a "real self" hidden inside which you can't express, and we can't meet?

This leads us to Problem #2:

Are your memories accurate, or do they have legs that spread into the future? Think of a person in your life who consistently badgered you or picked on you? I had a friend like that in elementary school. Her name was Doris. We hung out together in the 7th grade. She attached herself to me, I think, because I was an easy mark.

She could always make me cry, feel inferior, and dumb. She was a bully.

Fast forward to today (before COVID). I was at an event and talked to a woman who seemed pleasant, smart, and potentially fun to be around. Finally, we exchanged names and surprise, surprise, hers was Doris. My reminiscence of Doris #1 was so powerful that my interest in new Doris turned immediately to distrust the minute I heard her name.

The reverberation of the past has a hidden narrative that can affect your current behavior. I didn't even remember Doris#1 until the day after I met Doris #2. I just knew that she was off my list of potential new friends.

Our memories can be unreliable, especially when emotions are involved. How can we expect to have authentic conversations when we allow ancient memories to overtake today's interactions?

Thinking back, I realize that those hateful statements I was blaming on Doris#1 probably represented how I felt about myself at that point in my life and that I projected my feelings on to her.

"In order to cause a shadow to disappear, you must shine light on it." - Shakti Gawain.

Problem #3: Listening

Reviving our listening skills is critical to a good conversation.

What do you think about while another person is talking to you? Are you listening to what's being said, or are you focused on how you are going to respond? Chances are it's the latter. It's a common occurrence.

In a conversation, most people would rather be talking than listening. So, out of trying to be polite, we block our responses rather than simply blurting them out the minute they come to mind. Instead of hearing what our companion is saying, we are impatiently waiting for the other to stop talking so that we can say out loud what we have been silently rehearsing.

It might help to consider that the other person in the conversation is an expert at something, and you can be introduced to a new idea by paying attention. That might help.

Fruitful attainment of human to human communication can be achieved. It requires work from both the speaker and the listener. The speaker's work is to pay attention to what they say so that it's not repetitive or pedantic. The listener's job is to remain open to what is being said.

Here's a potential solution to these dilemmas. Pick a problem — #1)the dominance of our experiences, #2)memory influences, or #3)listening skills, and work on improving it. Building on any one of them can lead you to a greater appreciation of what you hear in your future conversations.

Give it a try. Your next partner in a heart-to-heart will notice you've been listening.

FOUR WAYS TO APPROACH EQUANIMITY
Despite everything occurring in our world, how can one search for inner calm?

It's always a good idea to start with a definition, so we know we discuss the same thing. You see, it's like being on the same page.

The definition of equanimity is evenness of mind, especially under stress. In a sentence, it could read like this,

"Nothing could disturb his equanimity."

In other words, like nouns, the difference between equanimity and passivity is that equanimity requires doing something to achieve calm, balance, and control. In contrast, passivity is the state of being passive. One is an active state while the other, an inactive one.

Indeed, to attain calmness in the state of our world today, we can turn to our inner resources such as:

Every hour or so, take time to sit down and experience your breathing.

You might even say a word to yourself (like "One," each time you inhale). Let your exhale be longer than your inhale. Exhale air and along with it, your sufferings. You might even allow yourself to verbalize a sigh. If you place one hand on your diaphragm area and the other hand on your chest, let your inhale move your lower hand first. Doing this will be sure to give you more air intake.

Remember that the one thing we can count on is "change."

No matter how impossible our situations are today, you can count on them not staying that way. Remind yourself that you have resolved problems before, and you can make resolutions happen again.

A personal challenge.

It has to do with becoming ill. In 1991, I was diagnosed with a chronic disease that changed almost every aspect of my life. It was such a blow that I went around for about ten years, feeling "subhuman." I felt less than everyone else because I needed (and still do need) a manufactured substance to keep me alive. Finally, with therapy, I accepted that while my situation was beyond stressful, I had to make it part of me. I began my search for peacefulness from the date I gave credence to my illness. I slowly built an animated image of myself that ultimately showed me to a state of equanimity.

Let's say that you are on the path of seeking calmness.

If you spend time judging yourself, you may wish to stop doing that.

It's OK to evaluate your state of being from time to time and celebrate the notion that any small advance to achieve serenity deserves a pat on the back. Here's how you do that: extend either arm out to the side, then cross it over your chest so that your hand goes over your opposite shoulder to your back. Apply gentle taps to the back of your shoulder.

This poem by the Sufi poet Rumi describes the challenge and the opportunity of living with equanimity:

THE GUEST HOUSE
This being human is a guest house.
Every morning a new arrival.
A joy, a depression, a meanness,
some momentary awareness comes
as an unexpected visitor.
Welcome and entertain them all!
Even if they're a crowd of sorrows,
who violently sweep your house
empty of its furniture,
still, treat each guest honorably.
He may be clearing you out
for some new delight.
The dark thought, the shame, the malice,
meet them at the door laughing,
and invite them in.
Be grateful for whoever comes,
because each has been sent
as a guide from beyond.

A DIFFERENT WAY TO FACE YOUR FEARS!
Try approaching scary things in a new way.

How would it feel if we approached every difficult thing in life with curiosity? We might ask ourselves, "what will it feel like while I'm presenting a report to 70 people?" Or, "what will the operating room in which my right knee will be replaced look like?" Or, "What will happen to me if I have to stay inside my apartment for another 8 weeks?"

What can be more challenging than life itself?

Philosophers, psychologists, and behaviorists have all suggested many techniques for successfully dealing with the stress accompanying life's challenges. We've heard about breathing techniques, physical activity, medications, listening to music, and many more. The Mayo Clinic defines three main types of stress relief: Autogenic Relaxation, which uses visual imagery and body awareness, Progressive Muscle Relaxation, slowly tightening and releasing muscles. Visualization, using mental images to go to peaceful places and then going there in our imagination.

Try this link for more information: https://www.mayoclinic.org/healthy-lifestyle/stress-management/basics/stress-basics/hlv-20049495.

Of course, any or all techniques that work for you are great. Here's a new one you may wish to try or add to your successful stress relievers. It's the Adventure Method (I've given it a name) that helps me: I consider every challenge which comes my way as a potential adventure. Adventures usually refer to fun trips we are going to take. But this method of stress relief engages your sense of adventure and converts any upcoming unknown experience into something that may be interesting. Once fear rears its ugly head, add curiosity. What will it be like to turn all upcoming potentially scary experiences into adventures? I've used this

Adventure Method many times in my life successfully. Here are some:

>Going to college and graduate school
>Becoming pregnant and being afraid to give birth
>Moving to Rhode Island and back to the NY area
>Divorcing my husband
>Marrying my second
>Moving from one apartment to another at the age of 86
>Having knee surgery

I've noticed that this works when I have decided to move forward even though the activity I'm moving to frightens me. As a little girl, I was frightened of everything, including the moon! I guess my survival depended on facing fear.

Give it a try! It may be just the stress reliever you need to add.

A FUN AND CAREFREE WAY TO FOLLOW A RECIPE!
It's your creation, so go for it!

I excitedly decided to make Jambalaya because I bought Andouille sausage. And, everyone knows that Andouille Sausage is a principal ingredient for that dish.

Right?

Cooking has always been an adventure for me, and also, I had nothing else to do! Jambalaya takes a long time to prepare, and I was all set to spend whatever time I needed to complete it. I didn't have all the ingredients, but that lack has never been my deterrent. That's where the adventure part comes in.

Here's what happened.

The first ingredient that I needed was bacon. I didn't have any.

The second ingredient was linguica sausage. I didn't have that either.

The next was Andouille Sausage, which, as I mentioned, I had.

These three ingredients were all to saute together without any added fat, rendering their own as they cooked, but I didn't have the fat-producing sausages. So I added some Olive Oil (not on the recipe) to keep the Andouille sausage from sticking to the pan.

The next ingredient was 4-5 cups of chopped onion. Well, I only had 2-3 cups, and I certainly wasn't going out to the store for more onions, so I used what I had.

Next was two chopped stalks of celery. Yeah, I had them.

Then came chopped red and green bell peppers, one of each. Instead, I had one red and one yellow bell pepper. I used them, of course.

These veggies were to soften while on top of the sausage.

Next came cut up chicken thighs, but I had chicken breasts. Not a biggie in the substitution department.

I had all the seasonings. Yeah!

Then, canned, diced tomato with green chilies was next up on the list. I had the right quantity of canned tomatoes but without the green chilies. Into the pot, they went anyway.

The recipe called for beef broth, but I only had chicken broth. So what, right?

Uncooked rice was next, but since I don't eat rice, I used Farro.

All this mixture then goes into the oven for 45 minutes.

Then, before serving, sprinkle the Jambalaya with chopped fresh parsley and chopped green onions. I didn't have fresh parsley, so I used dried. I didn't have green onions. Oh, well!

The Jambalaya was complete. It was yummy.

You probably have decided by now that this was a tasteless mess. But, to my surprise, it was delicious. I made so much of it; I brought most of it to my daughter's house for her family and they liked it, too.

I had so much fun while cooking this. I thought you might enjoy hearing about it. In this time of the COVID virus, having fun can come from an unexpected place. As you can see, substituting one ingredient for another is OK.

Don't be afraid.

A STEP-BY-STEP GUIDE TO BECOMING A BETTER LISTENER

*Improving your listening skills can overhaul your
relationships with friends and family.*

Listening is a skill that one supposedly learns throughout a lifetime. However, instead of listening, we tend to look as if we are paying attention when, instead, we are intensely busy planning what we will say next. And then, before you know it out pops our response, sometimes when our companion is still speaking. And, our answers are all about what we think they should do.

It happens to everyone at one time or another. Me, too.

Sometimes It's difficult for me to find the patience to listen to someone's entire story before I interrupt them with my solution. I feel terrible when I do this, but sometimes I forget how to be polite.

So here's a three-level listening scale to recognize our current practices and what may work better:

LEVEL 1

Listening to ourselves while another person is talking (a standard style.)

a) When we offer solutions, we assume they will help the other person, and, just as importantly, we are giving ourselves an unconscious pat on the back. When we offer a solution, we nourish our self-image of being kind, generous, caring, and smart.

b) We start the next sentence with the word "I," e.g., "I had the same thing happen to me." And then give all the details." This shift redirects the conversation from being about "them" to being about "you."

LEVEL 2

Listen to what the other person is saying (a rarer style.)

Offer nothing back except for maybe asking a qualifying question. Or become an active listener by acknowledging the emotion expressed by the speaker with kindness and empathy. You might reflect their emotion and say something like, "Sounds like you were annoyed." Or say nothing and give the speaker time to consider what they have just said.

LEVEL 3

Listening for the underlying thought, feeling, or origin of what was said (the rarest style.)

Eliminate our agenda, what we think and feel about our solution to their problem, so that it doesn't get in the way of hearing the speaker's truth. This last is not easy to do. I try to think of myself as an empty vessel from which I have poured out everything to allow the speaker and the speaker's point of view to be heard. I might say things like, "Tell me more."

Level 3 is the goal. Wouldn't it be great if we could all operate on level 3 listening;

World leaders might find ways to solve significant problems by listening to each other on a different level.

Families might be able to avoid the inevitable jealousy, hurt feelings, and insults.

Husbands and wives might be able to maintain the loving relationship they had when they married.

High school would be easy.

BECOMING AWARE OF HOW WE LISTEN NOW CAN LEAD TO ITS BETTERMENT IN THE FUTURE.

A TYPE 1 DIABETIC IN THE COVID-19 ERA

How my Diabetic journey controls my life.

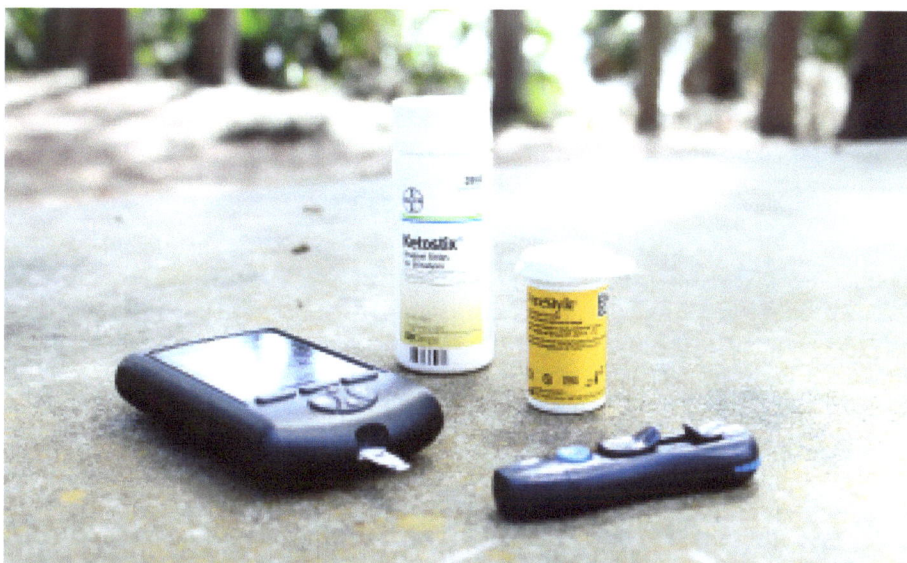

Today I learned from a study done by the United Kingdom National Health Service that Type 1 Diabetics are 3.5x more likely to die if they contract Covid-19 than Type 2's who are already twice more likely to die than the population that doesn't have Diabetes at all.

OH, GREAT!

You probably guessed that I am a Type 1 Diabetic. I was diagnosed when I was about 60, so it's been close to 30 years that I've been dealing with this 24/7 job of monitoring my Blood Glucose (BG) levels, taking my body with me when I go on vacation, eating healthy, and living a healthy lifestyle. You know, Type 1 Diabetes used to be called Juvenile Diabetes because it generally affected children. However, there are more exceptions to that rule, and visa versa; Adult Onset Diabetes is now affecting a younger age group. Pediatricians are now dealing with Adult Onset Diabetes patients, now called Type 2.

Type 1 Diabetes is an auto-immune disease in which the body's insulin-producing pancreatic beta cells are destroyed by the body's own immune cells by accident. Talk about mistakes; this one is a biggie. I've often said to my friends and family that this auto-immune stuff is the ultimate of self-hatred. I mean, after all, destroying one's own body, what else can one say about it! Of course, I'm only trying to sort of "lighten" this news, but most folks don't get the joke. Whoever said that to understand another person's trials fully, you must walk a mile in his shoes was right-on.

My life, since my diagnosis, has turned upside-down.

I feel like I'm living on the head of a pin, trying, sometimes desperately, to keep my BG in a narrow range, above 90 and below 150. While I strive to have complete control of this, I truly don't. Some factors that influence my BG levels go beyond my food and exercise choices, some internal, which can put my numbers over 400 and under 60. When I am out of control, I am filled with guilt. Since I have been using an insulin pump, I have much more precise control of insulin delivery. However, other factors that can negatively influence my BG levels include a bloody infusion site, bent inserters, an air bubble in the tubing.

On a personal level, I've lost a lot of spontaneity in my lifestyle. I've given up lots of food that I love, like pasta (at one point, I used to count out 14 strands of linguine as my portion), and try not to feel too sorry for myself.

Acceptance of what is — is the only option. An adage says something like — if you want to live a healthy life, develop a chronic disease, and take care of yourself.

Before I started using the insulin pump, I was on several insulin types, one of which needed to be injected 1/2 hr. before eating. The decision about exactly when to do this led to harrowing experiences. I was on a plane, and food was about to be served. I was seated in the front section of the plane, near the attendant's station, and I thought service would start at my end of the aisle. So, I injected myself, only to learn that food was served to the back of the aisle first and then slowly moved forward to where I was seated. I was panicked, thinking my BG would drop way too low before the food got to me. I survived but not without lots of anxiety.

So now, adding to my everyday anxiety caused by my BG life and times, the latest research mentioned earlier about Covid-19 and being a Type 1 Diabetic underscores my need to expose myself to other people as little as possible.

It doesn't sound like a lot of fun to me, but the other alternative of getting the Coronavirus is definitely worse.

CATCHY WAYS TO IDENTIFY YOUR NEXT CAREER
What Are The Qualities You Desire in Your New Job?

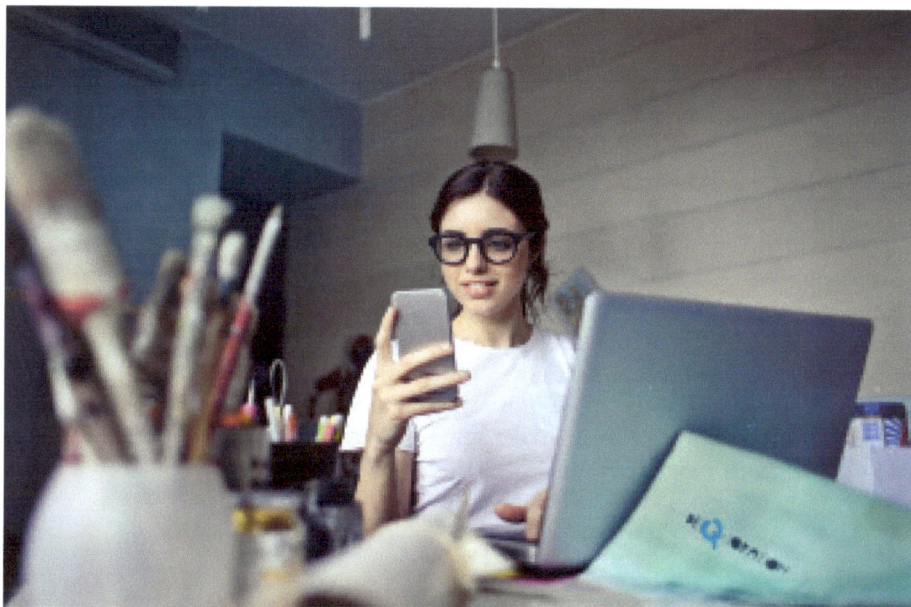

"WHAT MAKES YOUR HEART SING?"

How many of us are looking for a new job as a result of the Coronavirus lay-offs? Maybe we loved what we used to do and want to repeat that job or similar. But maybe, we feel like this is just the opportunity we needed to find something different to do in our daily lives. In other words, a new career.

But, doing what?

What will motivate you and make you happy? Consider:

Attainment/Fulfillment – enjoying stretching yourself when you undertake a difficult task — need to feel pride in using your skills —being challenged.

Being In "The Scene" – being involved and part of a high energy environment

Influential Leader – an opportunity to be recognized as a person with all the answers — setting the agenda for others — being sought out for the next step

Connections/People – Enjoying being part of a larger group, association, corporation, club, house of worship

Creative – needing an outlet for your creativity — think out of the box — be in an inventive environment.

Competitive – get energized by winning - compete for the prize

Each day your learning increases — continually expand your intellectual universe.

Current – Enjoy being at the cutting edge of fashion, news, electronics, thinking.

Improve the world – helping others, working for a cause — need to make a difference.

<u>Mentoring</u> – sharing yourself with a mind toward assisting another, usually a beginner

<u>Problem solver</u> – analyze where the heart of the matter lies and find solutions not seen by others.

<u>Visibility</u> – enjoy being in an environment where everyone knows your name.

<u>Acquiring Wealth</u> – working where the rewards are the highest, legal, and with the least hours – better known as PARADISE.

Think it over. Take your time and picture yourself in each of these environments. Where would you be most comfortable?

When you identify the one or two choices that turn you on, you can then determine which type of industry to seek employment. E.G., If your preference is Connection/People, you may wish to look for a job in a large corporation. And, if you also see yourself as a Problem Solver, you might aim for a job that encompasses this skill and is in a large association. Or, if your choice is being Creative, you might look for a job in a design studio or ad agency that's small enough to offer Visibility so that everyone knows your name.

On the other hand, if your preference is Acquiring Wealth, please let me know where your new job is, and I'll apply there, too!!!

DO YOU THINK EVER ABOUT YOUR VALUES?
Here's an enlightening way to rate your cherished inner standards.

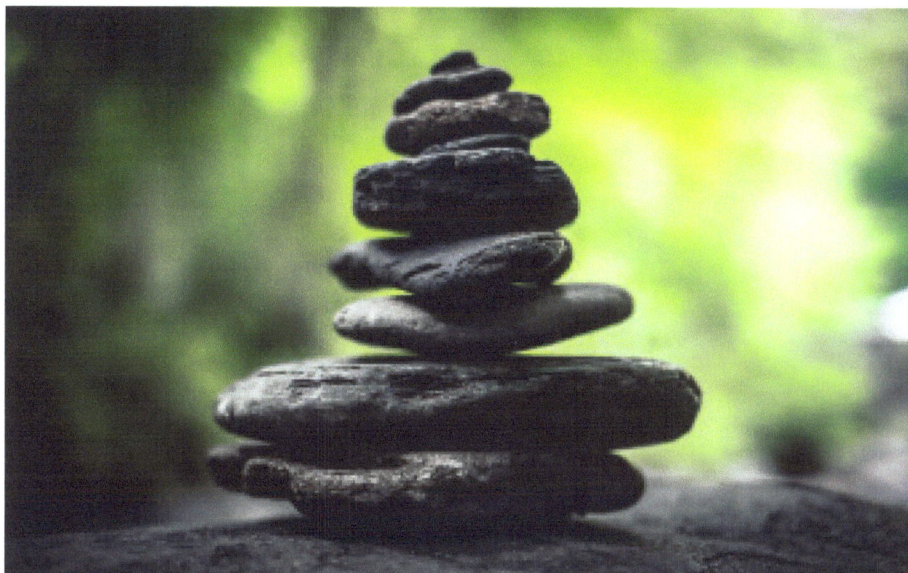

If you're mostly at home as I am, now would be a great time to think about your values. How about taking a look at what matters to you? You may have already created an inventory of your beliefs. That would be terrific!

But, if not, the following exercise will help you to identify values, which are your most treasured, and how much time you spend in your daily life actualizing them. For both columns, use a scale of 1–10, with 10 being the highest.

This little trick can make the following a useful exercise:

After filling in the "Rating" column, cover the numbers you've written. Then fill in the "Time Spent" column. Next, uncover your "Rating" and compare the numbers in each row. You will notice that they don't match, sometimes being more than five numbers apart. When you find those results or any that are greater than five, you will have uncovered the areas to work on to create your new reality. This exercise is a sequential process: 1) investigate, 2) identify, 3) take action.

Why crawl when you have a chance to soar?

I did this years ago and found that "Spirituality" was virtually non-existent in my life. So I started doing Yoga, and that helped. I also focused on "Self-Expression," about what I was feeling, and silently looked for the words to express the hidden part of me.

"Walking the Talk" was meaningful, too. The phrase alludes to living with authenticity, one of my goals in life.

After finding any of the values that need work, identifying what my feelings are about, and finding the words to understand them, I attempt to create an action every day that makes these discoveries part of me.

Give it a try. You might discover what you've been searching for — and, turns out, it's YOU!

Values Exercise		
Values	**Rating**	**Time Spent**
Accomplishment		
Abundance		
Adventure		
Beauty		
Commitment		
Communication		
Creativity		
Environment		
Family		
Flexibility		
Fun		
Honesty		
Humor		
Integrity		
Intimacy		
Leadership		
Loyalty		
Openness		
Orderliness		
Personal Growth		
Power		
Privacy		
Professionalism		
Recognition		
Respect		
Self-Care		
Self-Expression		
Service		
Spirituality		
Vitality		
Walking the Talk		

IS SAYING "NO" A NO-NO?
What are the risks and rewards of saying "NO" or "YES"?

Wait a minute! Aren't we supposed to be kind, loving, and accepting of the people we interact with every day of our lives? Haven't we been brought up to be patient, polite, and willing to listen to every word that comes out of their mouths? Is there ever a time that "no" is Ok?

When is it acceptable to say, "I'm done?"

Warren Buffet espoused the quick "no" and the slow "yes." In other words, think carefully before you say "yes" and commit your time and energy. For him, "no" must be easy, and "yes" the harder choice.

Let's look at some potential consequences of saying "yes" and saying "no" for the rest of us.

1. Starting from early childhood, parents trained us to obey them. There wasn't an option of saying "no" to a parent. If we tried it (and many of us did, including me), they could punish us for disobedience or worse. The worst might be a loss of approval from our parents. This painful consequence might result in a child growing up to be a People-Pleaser, who only feels good and safe if they are obedient to someone else's demands. The risk of saying "no" might lead to loss of acceptance and potential abandonment from Mom, Dad, or both. Later in life, happiness is only possible if everyone loves them.

A person with this disorder has a real problem in saying "no."

2. As we grow, being patient with someone can become a cumbersome habit. We can get so used to consenting to a friend's ask, saying "no" never enters our minds. If a friend or a family member needs us, we are ready and waiting to offer our assistance. But, once we become involved as a helper, our patience can grow thin.

Here's what may happen.

Sometimes the person in need realizes that our help is no longer required. They fear telling us for a variety of reasons. Maybe they think we'll feel unwanted, and their dismissal of us from the helper role can hurt our feelings. It could signal the end of the relationship.

But from our point of view, we would like it to be over. We have run out of patience and have found other demands on our time. What then? Our helper instinct is used up, but we are filled with doubt about the aftermath of our saying so.

What a predicament!

Both parties, due to fear of losing each other, are stuck. This is where courage is needed. They each need to be straightforward with each other. If the friendship is worth the effort, either party can take a risk and say "no more." End the helper/needer arrangement. That friendship will be sure to grow as a result. The "no" can be solid but said kindly. They will each develop greater trust in the truth of a future "yes" answer, and honesty will serve them.

What would you do, say "yes" or "no" in this situation?

3. What if you are in a work situation, and your boss asks you to do an assignment that you feel is above your current level of capability. Would you say "yes" or "no" to accept the task?

Look at this from the boss's side. He wants this job done and feels you are equipped to do it. How disappointed will he be by your refusal of the assignment? Will he have second thoughts about your ability? Will he reconsider your chances for future advancement at his company?

From your side, ask yourself, what if you say "yes" and then can't do the task. Discomfort takes over, even thinking about it. Are you exposing yourself to public failure and ruining your reputation? Or, if you say "no," are you ruining your profile anyway by not even trying? But what if you say "yes" and brilliantly complete the assignment?

How great would that be!

In this situation, it's always better to say "yes." You can always enlist help from co-workers or from outside the office to get the job done, if necessary. Challenging yourself results in your growth. Saying "no" may make you feel safer for the time being but will hold you back in the long run.

So, it's a mixed bag. There are times when "yes" is appropriate, and other times when "no" is a much better response. Of course, the best response is the one that reflects your authenticity and honesty. Give yourself time to respond when asked to do something. Try Warren Buffet's formula. That extra time gives you a chance to figure out how you want to proceed.

IS YOUR LIFE BORING LIVING DURING COVID-19?
Dealing with extra time and space can be challenging.

I've finally had to admit that living alone during Covid-19 is a lot harder than having a family or partner to share the everyday times when there is nothing to do. When I was little, I remember asking my sweet Grandma Esther, "What should I do now? I'm bored." (I was about 10.) She would always say, "Go to the corner and stand on your head." What I heard was that she wanted me to figure it out by myself.

Recently I've been speaking with many people, some who live alone and some who live with family but I hear the same complaint — nothing to do. And yet, there are others for whom the time flies by, and before you know it, it's time for bed. Which type are you? I think what it comes down to is what childhood lessons stuck with you. Along with that were your role models. How did your parents, your siblings, and your extended family and friends structure their lives?

If you're in the "nothing to do" group, this might be an excellent opportunity to re-think your approach to how you spend your time, therefore, how you spend your life. What if you took the time to ask yourself what your ideal life would be. Try being your fairy godmother; just imagine your perfect life. You might even write down your elements. Evaluate which ones are present right now and which are missing. Which is missing but crying out for some space?

Or you might answer the question, "Who Am I?"

On a blank piece of paper write down all the adjectives that describe you, the good ones and the bad ones. Then, evaluate which to enhance and which diminish.

Once you've done this, the next step is to figure out what you can do, in tiny in-crements, to modify the elements you want to enhance. Which of the qualities you've identified do you want more of in your life? Think about:

How would it feel to be in sync with this vision of myself and my life all the time?

Which of the qualities I've identified do I want more of in my life?

What have I wanted to do in my life but haven't dared to do it?

How am I going to accomplish what I need to do to be at my best?

So, you have now identified some changes you can work to be closer to whom you wish to be. Great start!

"Go confidently in the direction of your dreams." - Henry David Thoreau

L'SHANAH TOVAH! IT'S TIME TO HEAR THE SOUND OF THE SHOFAR

How comforting it is to hear its plaintive voice.

In today's world, one mostly hears the shofar only on the Jewish Holidays of Rosh Hashanah and at the end of Yom Kippur services, the end of Days of Awe. Once heard, it's hard to forget the power and ancient sound, and this is coming from an old French Hornist who recognizes instrumental power. So, you may ask:

What is a shofar?

A shofar is an ancient musical instrument made from a Ram's horn with no pitch altering device, much like today's bugle. All pitch altering comes from the player's embouchure or lip position. Shofars come in a variety of shapes and sizes and look scary and exotic.

Historically, the shofar was blown not only for religious occasions but for various other events as well.

Joshua, in his battle for Jericho, had the shofar blown to announce when the conflict was about to begin. The shofar was often taken along during a war in those primitive times. It was blown from a mountain top so that all could hear it as a call to arms. Many say that it was the shofar's call that assisted Joshua in his conflict to win Jericho.

And, ask yourself, what other means of communication were available?

The shofar has sounded as a sign of victory and celebration. Jewish elders were photographed blowing multiple shofars after hearing that the Nazis surrendered on May 8, 1945.

What does the sound of the shofar mean to you?

My friends and I were discussing what blowing the shofar meant to each of us. One friend said that it sounded like an alarm to her. We asked if she felt it was associated with some danger or an omen of something unfortunate about to start. She said she hadn't thought of it that way.

Another friend said that shofar blowing was meaningful to her because the sound relates to Jewish people all over the planet and reminds us of how connected we are to each other.

A third person (me) reflected on the ancient nature of the instrument and its distinctive sound. It doesn't have the melodic sweetness that other musical instruments have like a flute or violin. Its loud voice calls to Jewish people, reminding them of their ties to ancient times.

My ties to this instrument rest not only in its ancestral memory to Jewish universally but of much more recent events I experienced.

As a young girl, I lived amongst all my relatives. We each had a different address, but we were all within walking distance of each other. Our families got together almost every Saturday night to "hang out." The men sometimes played cards (mostly poker), and the women regularly enjoyed each other's company. As kid cousins, we giggled a lot and made up silly words and song lyrics for radio commercials.

But when the Jewish Holidays rolled around, things got more serious. It was necessary to discuss food, who was bringing what, and where we would eat it. Was it at Grandma's house again? Wouldn't someone step up and take over? My mother often did, especially after Yom Kippur, when we had a lavish feast of breakfast-type foods.

You can imagine what people are like after completing a 24-hour fast day — ravenous. Their much-anticipated food needs to be displayed and ready to be eaten, the instant everyone arrives back from the Temple after hearing the shofar's last blast.

The problem was someone had to put the food out at home, while the rest of the gang was attending the final part of the religious services. Well, who do you suppose was directed to do that job? It was my cousins and me, of course. As soon as we were old enough to get home on our own, we had to start removing the prepared food from the refrigerator. Platters of translucent, salty lox, bowls of thick white cream cheese, (plain or with veggies), vessels of tuna salad and egg salad, and baskets of bagels, of course, sliced, all of which had to be put on the table. We put juices and wines out for immediate imbibement.

On some level, we were glad to do it. Mostly it was because we could break our fasts sooner than everyone else since we dealt with all this food, but I paid the price. By being at home, I missed the last plaintive wail of the shofar, signifying Yom Kippur's end. As a result of being at home, I had to wait another whole year to hear it played again. I felt cheated from the sound which I loved and still do.

So you can see that my relationship with the shofar is ancient and personal. The old part is my Jewish heredity and the personal part, my longing to hear its last strains.

MY LAPTOP'S DESTINATION: THE GARBAGE PAIL
What I Learned While Dealing with a Computer Disaster.

If you're a senior and on your computer many hours every day like I am, I'm pretty sure you've run into unsolvable problems -like I did this past week. Here's what happened (it was dreadful!):

I keep a detailed list of bank accounts, credit cards, user names, car lease info, passwords, and other pertinent info about my life on my computer. I do this at the request of my children so that if I get sick (or die), they will know where the money is and/or how to take care of me.

The list has to be updated occasionally, as some credit cards are changed, sometimes new ones added, insurance companies sometimes come and go. All of this is normal.

On Friday, I was updating this list, and somehow I overwrote it with a story I had previously written on my blog. It was similar to having a cassette that chronicles a favorite event and then accidentally using the same cassette for another event. The second event eliminates the first one. The document's title is still accessible on my computer, but when I click on it instead of the directory, up comes my story's last page.

$@XDRAT&(&$#H GOD<O*&$#HELP&F — -&*&(00)

I'm 88? years old and have owned a computer since 1990, so computers are not strangers. Could this disaster have happened because I am old? Or did this happen just because weird things happen on computers?

Three years ago, I was able to switch from a PC to a MAC relatively easily. (I still use a mouse instead of the trackpad, and Apple has a nifty mouse.)

But my basic computer knowledge doesn't exist. I've always operated intuitively, even at my age.

I called my son, who is a software developer, for help. We tried several ways to overcome this problem, but nothing worked. The list is lost. Although my son was sympathetic, he told me that this sort of problem is usually caused by human error. Of course, I was ready to throw the whole laptop into the nearest garbage pail. Finally, I accept the fact that I DID SOMETHING THAT RESULTED IN THIS SITUATION.

Isn't it true that we will try arduously to blame something or someone else for our problems?

You know the thinking; I'm not responsible; I'm the victim here!

Luckily I have a paper copy of the list. Yeah! So my only reasonable but annoying choice is to recopy, manually, all that information, all those numbers, names, and passwords, back into the computer. The list is 5 pages long, and the opportunity for error is enormous. You may wonder why it needs to be computerized. The answer is that corrections are frequently required for accuracy, and a computer can accommodate changes more easily than writing notes in margins or crossing "stuff" out.

What a bummer! I'm now on page 3, working my way through to the end of it.

I know many seniors who have never laid a finger on a keyboard. I run into some serious computer issues from time to time, but my life is enlarged because of my use of this MAC. I would be lost without it. Google and other search engines increase the scope of my knowledge just by utilizing my keyboard. I'm still amazed by the vast amount of available information.

In researching the internet as preparation for writing this article, I came across an organization listed on Wikipedia that might help these seniors who have no computer skill. I have no relationship with the organization other than reading about it. So If you know any person over 55 who is afraid to try using a computer, you may wish to recommend this site.

SeniorNet is a 501(c)(3) nonprofit organization. "It is the nation's premier and most respected nonprofit organization" (according to them), specializing in computer and internet education for adults 55 and over.

There's a 2014 documentary film, Cyber Senior, directed by Saffron Cassaday. The film chronicles seniors' journeys as they discover the internet through the guidance of teenage mentors. Seeing it may encourage seniors who might otherwise be afraid to join the computer world.

What I recognized from this experience is that I will survive while accepting culpability for a mistake. My first instinct might be to put the onus elsewhere; I can work toward accepting responsibility for my actions.

NEXT TIME I'LL WIN FOR SURE!
Why are computer games so time-consuming and addictive?

Almost as soon as I owned my first computer around 1985, I discovered computer games. They were then such fun to play and remain entertaining today. Each game has a goal; you either win or lose. When you lose, you can try again immediately without any delay. It's not pleasant to lose. If you win, the reward is a sense of mastery over a silly time-waster, and an opportunity to play a more challenging game. This cycle is continual. There is always the "next" one ready to view and manipulate. These games feel innocent, usually not associated with any harmful substances, and not harming anyone.

So, what's the problem?

For many people including me, once you start, it's tough to stop. There are times that I've been late for appointments because I'm involved in a computer game. Also, I become angry with myself over my inability to walk away. I ask myself, "What's so great about this activity"? but get no answer.

I've developed burning sensations in my eyes from staring at my computer screen (or my iPhone screen) for such long periods of playing games. My ophthalmologist explained that one tends not to blink as much when staring at a computer screen for long periods, and one's eyes get dry with a burning sensation as a result.

So possibly, these games are not so innocent after all.

I researched gaming behavior and discovered a whole world of information, starting with B. F. Skinner's Operant Conditioning Theory.

Operant conditioning is a method of learning that occurs through rewards and punishments for behavior. Through operant conditioning, an individual makes an association between a particular behavior and a consequence (Skinner, 1938).

Skinner's theory explains that one learns that computer games offer rewards (winning the game) and punishment (losing the game). But wait, there are a lot of other factors that also figure into this behavior.

There is an article on the website "verywellMind.com" called; Reinforcement Schedules Are Used to Strengthen Specific Behaviors by Kendra Cherry Reviewed by David Susman, Ph.D. on July 24, 2020. You will find it under the 100+ Mental Health Topics tab. I suggest, if you, too, are suffering from computer game issues that you read it.

You will learn that if you are on a schedule of consistently winning or consistently losing, you will soon abandon the activity. What fun is it if you get the same result on every trial? Another type of boring outcome is, let's say, winning every fourth game you play. That game will soon become extinct.

Winning on a partial or variable reinforcement schedule causes the learned behavior to be strengthened and continue. In other words, it's the unknown factor of winning or losing, which is so entrancing that we MUST discover the outcome after playing the next, and next, and next game. And, since we have a history of winning unexpectedly once-in-a-while, we have learned that each game we play has the potential of rewarding us with a win. It's a brain function to seek pleasure, and winning feels good.

The power of Partial Reinforcement Schedules is essential to know. It extends to so many factors in our lives. If you are trying, for example, to start a business meeting on time with all staff members present, you might offer a reward such as an additional 15 minutes extension to lunch break the following day to a team member who shows up on time. The extra time is the reward. Do this every day until the staff expects this bonus. Then change the reward schedule and offer it unpredictably — the unknown factor of whether or not the team will receive the award will keep them showing up on time if the reward is meaningful enough.

OK, but how can I cure my video game addiction?

Currently, Cognitive Behavioral Therapy (CBT) is one tool that apparently can be effective. Also, group therapy can be a valuable source of moral support in understanding that you are not alone dealing with this problem.

I also looked to Google for assistance on where to find treatment centers near me. I found some close to where I live.

I'd like to tell you that I am actively seeking help, but that is not the case. So far, I'm gaining knowledge.

So, stay tuned.

SLEEP-DEPRIVED LOOK MAKE-UP IS THE LATEST!
A reflection about the connections between society and make-up.

Did you know that one of the earliest cultures to use cosmetics was ancient Egypt? Both men and women used make-up to enhance their appearance. In ancient Rome, Christian women tended to avoid cosmetics believing that they should praise what God gave them. However, even in those ancient times, make-up was a daily routine for wealthy women and prostitutes.

Of all the surviving texts mentioning cosmetics (all written by men), Ovid is alone in his approval of their use. The consensus was that women who used cosmetics in excess were immoral, deceptive, and were practicing a form of witchcraft.

Queen Victoria publicly declared make-up was improper, vulgar, and acceptable only for use by actors. Right after she died at the turn of the 20th century, Elizabeth Arden, Helena Rubinstein, and Max Factor developed their vast markets in the US during the 1910s, followed by Revlon and Estee Lauder, before and after WWII.

I was thirteen years old when my mother suggested I wear a little lipstick! I didn't want to put that greasy stuff on my face, but I must have been entirely unaware of how terrible I looked. Thinking back, I realize that I was overweight, had the shadow of a mustache, had one long eyebrow stretching across my face, and a few skin concerns.

My mother was making sure that my acne didn't get worse by insisting that as soon as I came home from school and before I did anything else, I had to wash my face with soap and the hottest water I could stand. After rinsing off the soap, I applied the washcloth to any area that already erupted or was about to explode in a pimple.

I followed this routine faithfully until I went away to college. In High School, I did anything my mother instructed me to do. Her wrath was not to be encouraged. One of her inhibiting methods was to discuss all of my embarrassing issues with her female relatives while I was present. My mother often referred to me as "she." It diminished me. How could I worry about lipstick or how I looked at all?

I was a meaningless creature. My role was to make sure I didn't embarrass Mom.

Finally, when I got to college, I reinvented myself. I can't imagine where I found the strength to do it. (I met a guy at a bar a few years later who told me I had a great "life force." Maybe he was right). I lost about twenty-five pounds during my freshman year, changed my hairstyle, and never wore make-up. And, my skin was smooth and soft.

It was like a miracle.

I must have used make-up during working hours after college and at my wedding. However, by the time I got married and had three children, I lived in Providence, R.I., where I wore no make-up except at fancy parties. One of my friends from Providence told a new friend from N.J., "Make sure Lynn wears make-up every day." My new friend agreed and nagged me about it continually.

And I started to wear make-up every day.

I wouldn't set foot out of the house without it. I wouldn't even step outside to get the newspaper without being made-up. I became addicted to wearing make-up. I fell in love with make-up. Many hours were spent at make-up counters examining new colors, changing my look from one year to the next according to the latest fashion, and getting instructions on applying it. It was all in the service of improving my appearance. And, make-up did just that!

In today's New York Times, Danya Issawi tells us that the make-up's most contemporary look is to darken the area below our eyes with brownish lipstick, the same place we used concealer on in the past to erase any discoloration. It's the sleep-deprived look, reflecting GenZ's insecurities. The look is the opposite of trying to look healthy during this miserable pandemic.

Today's world, with mask-wearing, has put a different slant on this situation. Sometimes I still wear eye make-up, but that's about it. I save tons of time, but then again, I have nothing to do and few places to go so the extra time serves no purpose. Masks are a significant Covid interference with regular life activities.

But that's just now; Eventually, Covid will pass.

I still love make-up and everything about it. It is fun to watch my transformation as I apply it. Wearing make-up is like a conversion into a new personality. It, too, is a mask but one of my choosing. I guess as soon as the Covid face-cover comes off, the make-up mask will return.

THE EBB AND FLOW OF EVIL
A story about seeking comfort wherever you can find it.

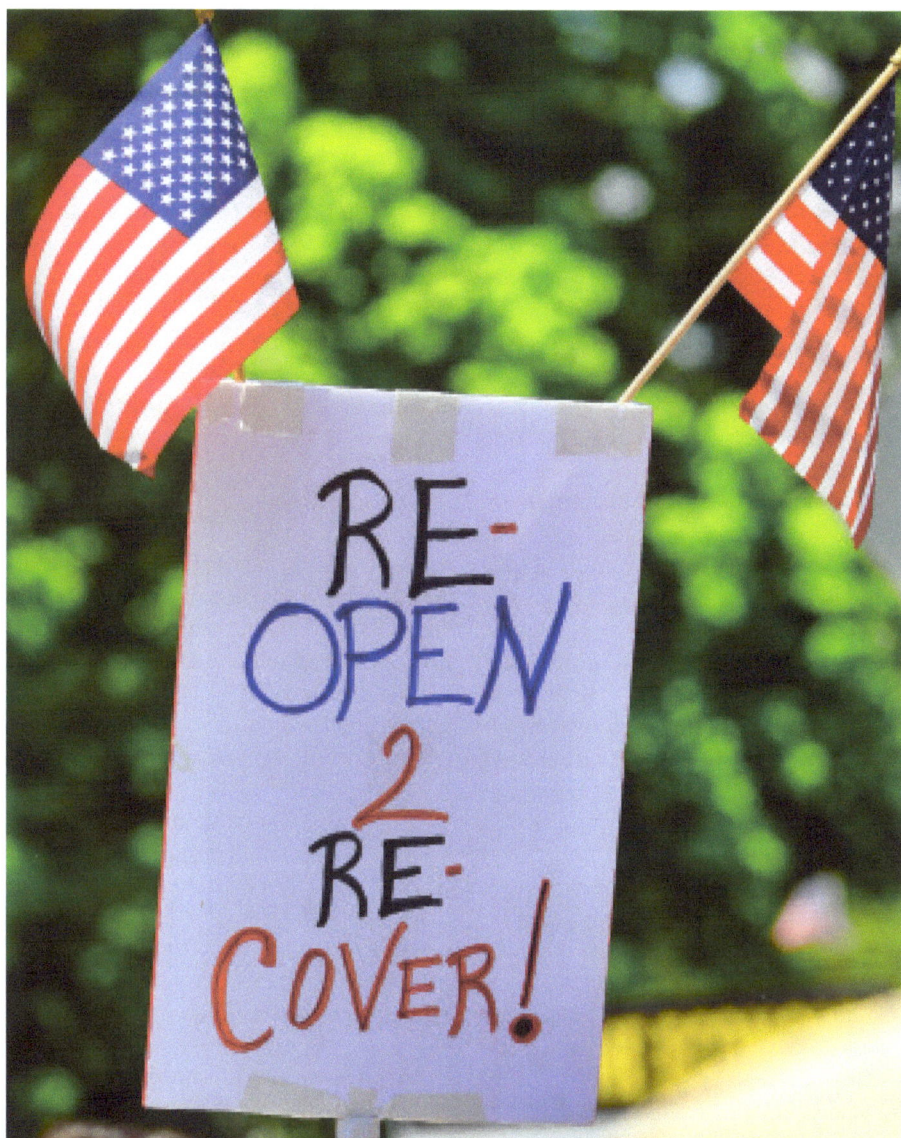

It turns out, everyone I've spoken to or read, even including writers for The New York Times, cried (or at least teared up) at the inauguration of Joseph R. Biden as President of the United States.

Of course, I was also one of the teary-eyed. Why was that?

After seeing all the horrifying pictures of the Capital two weeks earlier and having lived through the previous four years of warped leadership, it was overwhelming. The relief was palpable.

The U.S. Capital itself has grandeur. The flags filling the area that would, under normal circumstances, be people filled were playfully dancing in the gusts of wind. They seemed triumphant as if to proclaim that the good guys had won, after all. The words spoken on that day were powerful in expressing what is needed to return to our nation's former glory.

For me, the whole day validated my childhood sense of belonging to our mighty land, being proud of our values, and proclaiming to the rest of the world, "We have survived." I felt valued by the people in power.

I am just eleven years away from having lived for a century — a shocking realization.

I began to notice that during my lifetime, evil has arisen several times, as has good. The Great Depression was the backdrop of my birth. It ended as a result of good and evil. The New Deal was good, and WWII, for sure, evil. It was the war effort to manufacture supplies that finally lifted the yoke of the Depression.

After years of living through the anguish of the war came the marvelous post-war expansion enabled by the American GI Bill, allowing the average returning veterans to get educated, buy homes, and improve their lives. In Europe, there was the American Marshall Plan. There again, world affairs overturned from the worst to the best.

One could look at how circumstances repeatedly fluctuate from good to evil and back again throughout history, even from biblical times. It's the way of the world. We tend to forget about this in our everyday lives. When we're living through good times, we pretend they will last forever and the bad, like they'll be permanent.

We don't consider what comes next, and we shouldn't. As the saying goes, "Let the good times roll."

I used to feel that somehow if I didn't fully enjoy the good times, I could control the depth of the despair I felt from the bad ones. I had made a bargain with life. On balance, I thought if I experienced joy at about 80%, the upcoming pain would never get to 100%. I held back my pleasure as if to ensure my suffering in the bad times would be lessened. Surprise — that didn't work. Even though I put a lid on happiness, the bad times were still awful. The worst part of that bargain was tempering exuberance.

We might want to acknowledge that our darkest hours have the potential to be followed by the brightest. It's a way to find comfort and strength to help us through the worst of times. We all have them, so be on the lookout for signs of change.

Best advice: Try to remember, when you are at your lowest, the abundance of the universe will soon be knocking on your door.

Make sure to seek out and enjoy all the superior things that are present in our lives today.

WHAT WAS I THINKING!!
How a dearth of activity led me to an onslaught of stress.

When I moved into my current apartment two years ago, I spent as much money as the apartment cost modernizing it. I could hardly believe it until I summed up all my spending. While I completely renovated the kitchen, the bathrooms got short shrift — no new tile or plumbing, but new vanities, mirrors, and accessories. I thought it would do.

When the Master bath shower sprung a leak in the Fall of 2019 and thoroughly soaked the wall opposite the showerhead, I knew the "jig was up." It was time for a floor-to-ceiling makeover. So, I started interviewing contractors, and right after having the paint scraped off the wet wall, COVID arrived. That was the end of all serious renovations in my building — until recently.

I had to decide if I should convert this bathroom into a closet or fix the leak.

It seemed like fixing it would be a swell idea! With Covid-19 surrounding us and my being laid off from my job, I really didn't have enough to do anyway. Here was a project I could really dive into. I've explained in the past that activity is my tie to being connected to life around me.

Since February's COVID decree, other than having an outdoor meal with a few friends on occasion and seeing my daughter and her family once a week, I am in my apartment. I live alone. Most of my activities have been curtailed, as I'm sure yours have too.

As time goes on, I find myself tearing up more often, now even as I watch commercials in which two people are hugging. I keep tissues with me for face mopping. I've figured out that I am getting sadder and sadder, missing the comfort of touching and being hugged by another human being.

The answer came through loud and clear, REDO YOUR BATHROOM! (I must have been nuts that day.)

Well, deconstruction started last Tuesday. The first day was, as you would expect, very noisy and moderately messy. By the end of the day, all the old tiles, shower doors, and vanity were gone.

Then, on Wednesday, the back wall of the shower collapsed.

It seemed like the tile was holding up the wall rather than the other way around. Clouds of dust accompanied this event. It was like a gray cloud of particles descended into my apartment, leaving no surface unsullied. My shiny dark wood floors were gray with a matt finish. (Not the look I was used to.) The concrete dust found its way into every crevice and onto every surface.

And, of course, my contractor started muttering about how he would now have to rebuild an entire wall, not figured into the original price. So, the contract price went up to pay for the extra work. Actually, it wouldn't have been fair to him to include this extra work for nothing.

On Thursday, we expected the plumber, but he didn't come until Friday.

The contractor stayed home. I mistakenly didn't establish a price for the plumbing that had to be done in advance. I estimated it would be 2–3 hours of work to install a valve and redo the drain, but it turned out to be four hours instead. I had used this plumber before, and he had been reasonably priced. I expected the same treatment for this job. His hourly rate, however, had gone up since I last used his services. It turned out that he sent me his most lethargic worker, and the bill for labor was three times what the materials cost. It was outrageous. I'm trying to get it adjusted.

Stress, stress, and more stress has been my companion since then.

It arrives any time between 2:30 AM and 6:30 AM, signifying the end of sleep for the rest of that night.

I'm still hopeful that the result will be a pretty bathroom, worth all the money I've spent so far. But we still have a long way to go, so who knows what other problems may arise. When I dove into this project, I didn't expect to drown in it.

All I started out looking for was a non-leaky bathroom.

THE WORLD IS A WONDER
Advances have changed lives, like mine.

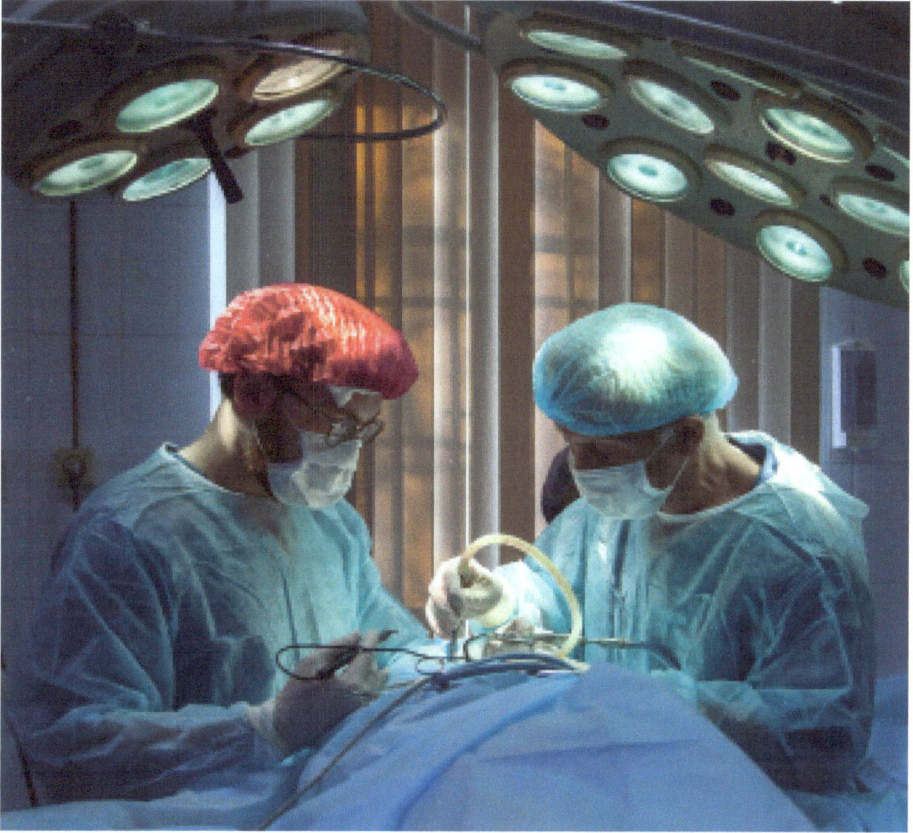

When we consider how the world is faring, we often forget how the effects of recent medical developments and treatment methods have progressed during the last fifty years.

A vaccine to prevent Polio was like a miracle. Every summer in my childhood, youngsters left cities to escape contracting it. We went alone to summer sleepaway camps or as families, rented a bungalow, or visited resorts in the Catskills and elsewhere.

There are now also vaccines for COVID-19, Measles, Mumps, and Rubella, treatments developed for AIDS, antibiotics, the creation of statins, atherosclerosis, and antipsychotic drugs. Advanced diagnostic tools, such as CT scans and MRIs, became available. The ongoing Human Genome Project is expected to uncover other amazing treatments and knowledge.

In 1957, my husband, a Type 2 diabetic, had to boil his syringe to sterilize it in preparation for his daily insulin injection. There was only one type of insulin available at the time. ACCORDING TO WIKIPEDIA, Frederick Banting and Charles Herbert Best, working in the laboratory of J. J. R. Macleod at the University of Toronto was the first to isolate insulin from a dog's pancreas in 1921.

The type of insulin my husband took peaked in efficacy at about 6:00 PM every day, so if dinner was delayed, he became increasingly hypoglycemic (blood glucose below normal), cranky, childlike, stubborn, and aggressive.

It was hell to manage his mood swings.

I was diagnosed with Type 1 diabetes in 1991, and by that time, the diabetes world had made great advances. In 1924, Becton Dickenson developed the first disposable insulin syringe, but they weren't popular until WW11 spurred their use for the battlefield. Isn't it strange when a war produces good things!

Disposable syringes were readily available when I needed them. The insulin world developed new insulin varieties, so combining them at different times and amounts resulted in precise insulin delivery for maximum blood glucose (BG) control.

I injected myself multiple times each day and carried syringes, insulin, and food with me at all times. I still carry food for emergencies, but the insulin delivery is automated. My diabetes is a 24/7 responsibility to my health and will always be so.

I became an insulin pump user in 2003.

My lifestyle improved at once—no more multiple daily injections. The pump requires one injection every two to three days, and its precision is unbeatable. The first insulin pump was developed in 1974.

Another vast improvement came with using a Continuous Glucose Monitor, which delivers BG readings painlessly. Every finger was black and blue from continually jabbing my fingers for blood samples. And the pain seemed to increase as time went on before I embraced the new technology.

Compared to boiling syringes, my diabetes care has improved enormously. I am so thankful for these advances. My life, while not normal, is a closer facsimile. And, I have other issues to be thankful for, as well.

I have an Essential Tremor that was getting out of control.

My shaking hands interfered with getting food into my mouth as control became harder and harder, and my handwriting deteriorated to illegibility. My life was transitioning into living hell.

I found a neurologist who treats movement disorders with Botox. I was praying it would help, but the jury was out. I had my first treatment and, on a scale from 1–10, moved from a "2" level of discomfort to a "7" of comfort. My improvement is significant. I can hardly believe that Botox did it. The other treatment options for Essential Tremor are scary. Hurray!

Botox is so simple, injections every three months. What could be easier?

However, many challenges in the medical world remain unmet, including the appearance of antibiotic resistance, the obesity epidemic, and we can't forget the spread of COVID-19. Are we prepared for the next inevitable pandemic?

All-in-all, the world is advancing wildly every day. What with all the pain we have endured from living with the COVID plague, if we look at the big picture and examine blossoming research and its ultimate enhancement of our daily lives, we can rejoice. If we have accomplished so much in the last fifty years, think how much is yet to come in the next period.

Be happy and thankful that things are so great now.

HOW LONG SINCE YOU HAD A TANTRUM?

Here's a way to have this fun experience and more.

HAVE A TANTRUM to remove stress.

While tantrums are usually associated with children's confronting uncontrollable anger or frustration, having a tantrum on purpose can be a great liberating experience for an adult.

Here's a tip: Do this when you are alone at home without being inhibited by family and when you feel that existence is a sad slog, or your life is undergoing a torrent of experiences you can't control. In other words, a tantrum may erase a bummed-out feeling.

Ruthy Alon, a disciple of Moshe Feldenkrais, creator of the Feldenkrais Method, describes how to do it. The Method encourages gentle, mindful movement to bring new awareness and possibility of movement into every aspect of your life. But, there is little that's gentle and mindful in having a tantrum. It is designed to remove control.

First, lie down on the floor, with or without a pillow under your head. I do it without because I feel it gives my head a chance to line itself up with my spine.

You can also do this while seated in a chair or lying on your bed.

Start by bending your knees to make your feet flat on the floor, about hip-width apart, arms down the sides of your torso. Then start to move your right foot up and down as if you were walking.

Stop that and switch to the left foot with the same up and down movement, then alternate from one foot to another. Leave your legs in this position, resting.

Next, move your right forearm and hand up and down. Position your hands in soft fists. Do this about five times. Then do the other side the same way. Now, start moving your entire right arm and shoulder, up and down a few times, and then the left side. Alternate the right and left sides. Now, gently turn your head to the right and left without lifting it.

Now, you're ready.

Start to move everything, arms, legs, and rolling your head all at the same time. Increase your speed to frantic and at the same time shout, "No, No, No" for as long as you like. You'll get the gist of this right away. Take a rest, and when you're ready, do it again, this time shout, "Yes, Yes, Yes."

I liked "No, No, No" better than "Yes, Yes, Yes." It released a load of pent-up anger.

You've done it. You've had a tantrum. How do you feel?

ALIVE AND IN LIVING COLOR another stress remover.

Here's another unique way to relieve stress. MICHAEL BIAS, ARTISTIC/ PRODUCING DIRECTOR, my acting coach/teacher, described this path.

Pick a color. Any color will do.

Sit comfortably in a chair and imagine that this color fills your body starting from your head. Feel the color as it fills your forehead, face, neck, shoulders, down your arms to your fingertips. The color moves slowly, so don't rush.

It continues filling your chest, abdomen, pelvis, down your legs to your littlest toes. Rest there for a few minutes allowing yourself to luxuriate in this color.

You are no longer just you; now you are a color radiating love, magnificence, and a richness absent before.

Next, imagine that a small hole has opened in your toe, and the color slowly starts to leave you. First, your head and face return to how they usually feel, and gradually, slowly, your whole body is being reborn. You are at rest, peaceful, calm, and ready to tackle a challenge.

You can do both of these exercises. Even if they are out of your regular range of activity, you'll find they are rewarding. Be fearless and daring. The result will be worth it.

THE END

ACKNOWLEDGMENTS

Throughout this process, there has been no one as supportive as my daughter Ruth. She supported me when I became discouraged, and has helped unendingly in the publication of this book, going so far as completing computer requirements that stumped me. Thank you, Ruth, my right and left hand.

As a new writer, I sought feedback wherever I could find it. I was inexperienced and needed help. Searching around on the internet, I found Grammerly.com, an online company that reads every word I write, and corrects grammatical errors. I became a customer of theirs. Thank you, Grammerly.com.

Writing a book is a process. First, comes the actual writing which is solitary, and fun. My process has been a week- to- week event, taking up only about half a week for each article. As they began to accumulate on my laptop, I mentioned them to my son, Eric, a knowledgeable computer guy who recommended me to Medium.com. He also directed me to valuable resources on How to Self Publish. Thank you, Eric.

As time went on, my friend, Dr. June, who read my blogs, suggested that I submit them to media outlets for publication. I was flattered, surprised and tried a few submissions. None was successful but it was a half-hearted attempt on my part. I just couldn't see it happening. Then she suggested that when I'm ready, I might combine all finished articles into a book, get it published, and present it as a legacy to my friend and family. I thought that was a lovely idea and as you can see, have done it. Thank you, June.

My friend, Nikki, who reads every blog I write, and gave me much needed feedback, noticed a writing course offered online. Thank you, Nikki. The online course, Memoir Writing, Ink, is taught by Allison Wearing. I took the course and learned how to make my words come alive. Thank you Alison.

My friend, Alice, also reads my blogs and has put up with my using her, un-named, of course, as the target of some topics she has engendered. Thank you, Alice. You're a good sport.

My graphic designer, Sally Diaz, of Blackswift Creative designed my cover and formatted my book. She is outstanding, talented and kind, all qualities I admire. Thank you, Sally.

My son, Pesach, reads my blogs and engages with me in discussions about their meaning. Many of them are regarding things that happened during his childhood. He is my oldest child, and has memories of things I mention. Thank you, Pesach.

My friend and son-in-law Alan, is so supportive of my effort. He's been my link to Linked-in and always listens to my complaints and frustrations, being helpful without overbearing. Thank you, Alan.

I've been encouraged by many friends, Elizabeth, Sheila, Robin, Lois, Delly, Joan, Fran, John, Miriam and everyone who took time to let me know they read my blog. You can't imagine how meaningful it was for you to have read what I wrote and let me know. Thank you.

www.ingramcontent.com/pod-product-compliance
Lightning Source LLC
Chambersburg PA
CBHW042125080426
42734CB00001B/1